THE ABC'S OF
SPECIAL NEEDS PLANNING
MADE EASY

"This book is more than just another guide on planning for the future. It is easy to understand and is full of great examples. Bart covers all of the major issues for families to do future and special needs planning. I have added this book to my 'must read' list for families. Most families don't like to think about the time when Mom and Dad are no longer there to care for their loved one with special needs. But this book helps a family walk through this process. And, let's face it, no one offers the level of care that Mom and Dad does, but with good detailed planning, parents can rest assured that their child will receive quality care. Bart addresses the true quality of life concerns that all families face on a daily basis. I personally believe that Bart is on a mission to ensure that all families with special needs children complete high quality planning for the future. This book and *The Special Needs Planning Kit*, are the tools that every family needs to achieve their planning goals."

> — Craig C. Stoxen, *President and CEO*
> *South Carolina Autism Society*
> *Columbia, South Carolina*

"What magnificent work. I am absolutely thrilled that I'll be seeing this on the bookshelves. I will finally be able to refer something great to the millions of people who need it. Truly, truly, thank you for writing this book. *The ABC's of Special Needs Planning Made Easy* is an outstanding guide for parents and professionals who are providing future planning services to those with extra challenges and their families. You will reach for this invaluable book again and again. Thank you Bart Stevens for sharing your practical advice, experience and wisdom with all of us."

> — Judith Loseff Lavin,
> *author of SPECIAL KIDS NEED*
> *SPECIAL PARENTS: A Resource for Parents*
> *of Children with Special Needs*

"Having known Bart for several years, we have always appreciated his writings and guidance in future planning. As parents of a child with a disability and as professionals working with the special needs population, we have found Bart's work to be inspirational and informative. This step-by-step book turns a vital and complicated process into a workable course of action. *The ABC's of Special Needs Planning Made Easy* will be an invaluable resource for our firm and our clients."

— Gregory M. Zibricky, *CFP, ChFC, CLU - President*
— C. Dawn Zibricky, *RN, MS, CSN -*
Special Needs Consultant
Provider Group, Ltd.,
Burr Ridge, Illinois

"Bart has succeeded admirably in the difficult task of writing an indispensable handbook for parents to understand and effectively complete a complex process. His style is clear and easy to understand with his step-by-step process. This book clearly defines not only how to protect your special needs child today, but for life. A 'must read' for every parent with a child with special needs."

— Judee Samuels Podvin
University of Central Florida - Center for Autism
and Related Disabilities
Orlando, Florida (UCF-CARD)

"I first met Bart Stevens in February 2002 when I flew to Phoenix to meet with him and attend his seminar. Our meeting was the culmination of a six-month long search, looking for answers to a very personal special needs situation. The search began as a result of my brother's death from a freak mountain bike accident. During the process of settling his affairs, which involved an adult child with special needs from a previous marriage, it was discovered that the planning protocols in place, were the exact opposite of what was required in circumstances involving a special needs child. Fortunately, Bart possessed the expertise that was not readily available in my local estate planning or legal community. As a financial advisor myself, I still needed assistance and am grateful for Bart's caring and professionalism."

— *Wally Pihl*
The Planning Group
Half Moon Bay, California

"As an attorney and the father of a child with special needs, *The ABC's of Special Needs Planning Made Easy* contained all the information I needed in order to prepare the most secure and comfortable future plan for my daughter. Her SSI benefit had been reduced by one-third because, as an adult over age 18, she was living at home and not paying any rent. By following the advice in the book, I was able to increase her benefit to the full maximum allowed. I would encourage both families and professionals in this Field to read this excellent book."

> — *Jeffrey R. Feller, Attorney At Law*
> *Feller Law Offices*
> *Phoenix, Arizona*

"My husband and I had the pleasure and fortune of meeting Bart at our State's annual Autism Conference. At first we were skeptical about the subject matter and topic of conversation. Who wants to think about passing away? Furthermore, why should we start planning when our child is only four years old? The subject matter aroused our curiosity. Perhaps we could learn something new.

We decided to attend Bart's presentation and it turned out to be one of the smartest investments of time that we could have ever made for our daughter, who has autism, as well as for our two other children.

Bart presented the subject matter in an easy-to-follow, understandable format. We were shocked and surprised to learn about how deeply our child could be affected by our passing away without the proper preparations. Following his presentation, we immediately consulted with Bart for help in preparing our Special Needs Trust, along with our attorney. Since the completion of our Trust, we feel as though a large weight has been lifted from our shoulders. We find comfort in the fact that in the event of our passing, our child will be well cared and provided for, thanks to Bart's assistance in planning.

> — *Cheryl A. Bauerle, Vice Chair*
> *South Carolina Autism Board of Directors*
> *Myrtle Beach, South Carolina*

THE **ABC**'s *of* SPECIAL NEEDS PLANNING

...*made easy*

BART STEVENS, ChLAP

Published by The Stevens Group, LLC
Phoenix, Arizona

Publisher:
The Stevens Group, LLC
12406 North 32nd Street, Suite 102
Phoenix, Arizona 85032

If you are unable to order this book from your local bookseller, you may order directly from Bart Stevens Special Needs Planning, a dba of The Stevens Group, LLC.
Quantity discounts are available. For information contact:

BART STEVENS
special needs planning

12406 North 32nd Street, Suite 102 • Phoenix, Arizona 85032
Voice: 602-404-4239   Toll Free: 888-447-2525   Fax: 602-996-0944
www.BSSNP.com
E-mail address: info@BSSNP.com

Library of Congress Control Number: 2002095241

ISBN: 0-9725642-0-9
First Printing/November 2002
First Edition
Printed in the United States of America

Cover and Book Design by: Creative Syndicate, Inc.

for Barbara

TABLE OF CONTENTS

S T O R I E S

H I N T S

ACKNOWLEDGMENTS

Although a book is typically authored by one person, there are other people who play important support and advisory roles, but remain in the background. First and foremost, I want to thank my wife, Barbara. A published author in her own right, she made the writing job far easier and less time consuming than if I had to do this on my own. Without her, this book would not have been possible. Along with Kirsten Adams, our Marketing Consultant, these two incredible women allowed me to concentrate on writing, while they took over the day-to-day responsibilities of running our business and making all the necessary arrangements to get this book published. I am grateful for their sacrifices and support.

A very special thank you to Jim Pavletich. Jim is a Technical Advisor with the Social Security Administration office in Mesa, Arizona. He has almost 30 years of experience with them. I met Jim about ten years ago when I first became involved in special needs planning. Over the years he has always been available to give me the necessary time to answer my questions and provide information. Countless times, he has helped my client families work through problems they have encountered trying to meet Social Security eligibility requirements for their children. His assistance in checking the accuracy of the Social Security information herein has been invaluable. Jim exemplifies the qualities of a truly dedicated government professional who all too often do not receive the praise and recognition they so justly deserve. He has, and continues to be a great mentor and teacher.

Since 1993, when I began special needs planning, I have had the good fortune to meet, speak, and work with many wonderful people who make up this unique community. My relationships with support groups and organizations, attorneys, financial advisors, government agency personnel, teachers, medical practitioners, therapists, families and persons with special needs over the years, has provided much of the information contained in this book. To all of you, my sincerest and heartfelt thanks.

ABOUT THE AUTHOR
BART STEVENS, ChLAP

Bart has been providing estate planning services since 1972. He is a graduate of Fairleigh Dickinson University, Madison, New Jersey and a U.S. Army veteran. Bart founded Bart Stevens Special Needs Planning in 1993 exclusively to educate, provide information, and assist families in planning for the future care, supervision, and security of their loved one with special needs. He is one of the first planners to have earned the professional designation of Chartered Lifetime Assistance Planner (ChLAP) from the National Institute on Life Planning for Persons with Disabilities.

In 1979 he and his wife, Barbara, moved from Morristown, New Jersey to Scottsdale, Arizona where they reside with their two dogs. Barbara is also an author whose first book, *Not Just One In Eight - Stories of Breast Cancer Survivors and Their Families* was published and released nationally in October 2000.

Bart is a nationally recognized speaker at local, state, national and international conferences. These organizations include the National Autism Society of America, National Down Syndrome Society, National Down Syndrome Congress, National Spina Bifida Association, and TASH. He also conducts educational seminars, provides individual planning assistance and group planning workshops throughout the United States. He has written articles for publications including *The Advocate* (The Autism Society of America's newsletter) and *Paraplegia*

News. He has been a guest on radio and television shows. He has also been interviewed by *The New York Sunday Times* (1/9/00); *Mature Outlook Magazine* (12/00); *Kiplinger Reports* (Fall 00); *The Washington Times* (3/27/01); and *The Chicago Tribune* (10/01). Bart authored the Life Planning brochure for the National Down Syndrome Society. He is the creator of *The Special Needs Planning Kit©* do-it-yourself planning system. He has worked with hundreds of organizations, support groups, government agencies, school districts and professional groups nationwide.

CREDENTIALS

Chartered Lifetime Assistance Planner (ChLAP)

Executive Director — Bart Stevens Special Needs Planning

President & CEO — The Stevens Group, LLC

Fellow — The National Institute on Life Planning
for Persons with Disabilities

AUTHOR'S MESSAGE

Dear Reader:

Thank you. Not as much for buying this book, but for taking the first step in learning how to plan for your loved one's future. I know it is a difficult subject to address and the last thing you want to do is read a lengthy and technical piece on planning. Since 1993, my experiences speaking before thousands of families at conferences and seminars, and more importantly, listening to what they had to say through their questions and comments, made it clear what information was needed in this book and how to present it.

This book is not just for family members. If you are an attorney, financial advisor, insurance agent, case worker, physician, therapist, teacher or any other professional providing services to people with special needs and their families, this book will be invaluable to you. In order for families to create the best possible plan for their loved one, it is important that the process be coordinated amongst all advisors and providers. With this information and knowledge, it will help you to better understand the many issues in planning that may not normally be a part of your typical work. However, you will see how the many aspects in planning affect each other. The information is intended to help you be a better and more knowledgeable planner or care provider.

The ABC's of Special Needs Planning Made Easy © identifies the many issues and concerns families like your's have, or will experience. You will learn how to resolve these issues in an easy to understand format. I will explain the consequences if you do not plan. Your State and Federal government already has a plan for your child that you will not like. However, now you have the opportunity to replace it! This book is arranged so you may quickly refer to a particular topic. Stories are included portraying true life situations. You will also read helpful "Hints" to assist you in the process.

With any task you do, whether it is preparing a meal, planning a party, fixing the lawnmower or making a model plane, it is always easier and usually gets done correctly, if you follow a step-by-step method. Not having instructions could also increase the time it takes to cook that meal or build the model plane. This also applies to special needs planning. That is why you will be introduced to a simple *Ten-Step Planning Process* that guides you from starting your plan to finishing it in a relatively short time and at an affordable cost.

I am always asked after a presentation to a group, "Okay, now what do I do to begin?" One thing for sure is I do not want you to delay starting your loved one's plan when you have finished this book. With millions of families having the same needs, there aren't enough planners qualified to personally assist each of you. In many cases, with the proper tools, most families will not need start-to-finish assistance from an attorney, accountant or financial advisor, although each of these professionals have an important role to play in the planning process.

My goal is to educate families so they can be in charge of the planning process and direct their advisors as to what they want, not necessarily what the advisor says they should do. To compliment this book and fulfill that goal, *The Special Needs Planning Kit©* was created and introduced nation-wide in December 2001. Details and information about this do-it-yourself system are included in Chapter 8. Together, *The ABC's of Special Needs Planning Made Easy©* and *The Special Needs Planning Kit ©* provide the simplest, most affordable, and time saving way for you to create the plan that you want for your loved one.

The Kit has also proven to be an invaluable tool for attorneys, financial advisors, and insurance agents as both a guide to planning with their clients and having the families complete the data forms themselves. All the information the attorney and advisors need in order to assist families in completing their plan is provided through the Kit. A sample Special Needs Trust is also included.

In order to provide in-depth information on the many subjects discussed here, it would take a multi-volume encyclopedia type text. This would be impractical and you probably would not want to read it. I want you to be able to read through this book in an evening or two and begin planning. There will be topics that you will want and need more detailed information about. Some subjects require that you obtain your State's specific guidelines. Examples would be information on guardianship, Special Needs Trusts, and government entitlements. References for this information are listed in the *Resource* section of this book.

While this book focuses on Special Needs Planning, it is important to coordinate this plan with your "traditional" estate planning. Family income needs for a surviving spouse and all children, education funding, and your retirement planning should not be overlooked. This type of planning will require the assistance of an attorney, financial or insurance advisor, and possibly a tax consultant. Chapter 6 gives you advice and guidance for the process of finding, interviewing and selecting your advisors.

Planning for the future of your loved one with special needs is no longer an option. It is a critically important responsibility. It *can* be done and you *can* do it. Use this book as your partner in planning.

Before you proceed, make sure you have a pen and pad handy. You are going to think of questions for your advisors and Social Security. Write them down as you think of them. Many will be answered as you read through the book.

Let me be the first to congratulate you for making a commitment to provide one of the most important and beneficial gifts you will ever give your loved one. Your legacy and your love.

Sincerely,

Bart Stevens

I N T R O D U C T I O N

Can you imagine leaving your child in someone's care for just a few hours without giving them any detailed instructions on what his or her needs are; what to do; how to do it; who to call in a medical emergency or how to reach you? You would not conceive of doing such an irresponsible thing to your child with special needs. However, this is exactly what you are doing if you have not prepared a plan for their future care, supervision, security and quality of life when you are no longer here.

Yes, this is a difficult subject that no one wants to discuss, but the reality is that you may not always be here because your child will probably survive you. You will not be gone for "just a few hours." You are gone permanently!

Stop for a minute and think about what would happen if tomorrow morning you are not here. Review all the things you do each day for your loved one. Dressing; feeding; getting them off to school, work or the adult center; knowing their dietary needs; how to communicate; and all the other "little" details. This information must be given now to current providers (teachers, therapists, medical practitioners, case workers) and those who will serve in the future (guardians, trustees, conservators). Do you want the people who provide care and protection for your child to have to figure everything out on their own? What effect will this have on them and your child? Is it fair to them or your child not to plan now before it is too late?

When the parents of a child with special needs passes away, the child is going to face a difficult and challenging transition. It could include moving to a different home; attending a different school or adult center; having to give up their job; leaving friends and all the other things that makes them comfortable and secure. Only you have the ability to make this transition as easy as possible for your loved one and the people who will be providing care and services for him or her. Would you want it any other way?

Do you want to decide who these future care providers will be? Do you want to decide how much of your estate will be left for your child? Do you want to run the risk of your child forfeiting government benefits and having to payback the government for benefits already received from assets you leave them? Of course you don't. If you have done no planning, you will learn about the plan your State and Federal government has for your loved one. Rest assured, you will not like it.

The purpose of this book is to educate and assist you in identifying the common issues and concerns all families must address, and to provide solutions and the means to eliminate these concerns so you can be assured your loved one will have the best care, security, and quality of life.

Though filled with a great deal of information, this book is presented in a concise and easy to understand manner. It is unlikely that you will find this scope of up-to-date information in one text.

Concerned? Worried? Want to be sure that your child is cared for by people you choose? Want to be sure your child receives loving care? Do you want to make the decisions for today, tomorrow and the future? I'm sure you do. You wouldn't be reading this book if you did not.

Here are some disturbing statistics to think about.

★ People with disabilities are two and one-half times less likely to be employed than persons without a disability.

★ About one-third of all people with disabilities are trying to make ends meet with a poverty level annual income of less than $15,000.

★ Approximately 20 percent of the U.S. population has some type of disability. More than half are classified as severe.

★ These numbers are growing at a rate of three percent per year.

Over the years, I have learned some very helpful "Hints" regarding various issues in planning. This includes information from families, professionals and government agency officials. You will read these "Hints" throughout this book.

When you finish, you will know what to do, how to do it, and be able to begin an organized, time saving, comprehensive, affordable, step-by-step method to be assured that your child will have the best future possible, and to give you peace of mind. In Chapter 8, you will learn about the do-it-yourself *Special Needs Planning Kit*© which contains the information and forms needed (including a draft for the Special Needs Trust) to complete the *Ten Simple Planning Steps* described in Chapter 4.

C H A P T E R   O N E

Why You Should Plan

In 1950, the life expectancy of people with special needs was about 30 years. Today, most expect to live a normal life span. The point to be made here, is that your loved one will probably survive you.

In past generations, families rarely made any plans for the future care and supervision of their loved one because the person either died before the parents, or they were placed in institutions which took full responsibility for their care. Many Mom's and Dad's of children with special needs, relate how doctors would tell them to "put your child in an institution and forget them." Not knowing what else to do, many did just that thinking it was best for their child. Professionals and families have learned that this was not always the right solution.

As typical children grow and mature, families look for their special talents and abilities and provide encouragement to pursue them. In a parent's mind, a child who can hit a baseball with ease may be a future Hall of Famer; one who draws well may be the next Picasso; the one who loves to cook may be the next Emeril. All parents have dreams about what their child's future will be like. A typical child can choose their own career path in life. Children with special needs also have *abilities* and can do many enjoyable and productive activities. Shouldn't they be allowed to try different things and take advantage of every opportunity available?

What dreams and wishes do you have for your child? Does your child have dreams and wishes of their own? Have you asked your child what they are? Have you shared them with others? What plans have you made to be sure that your child will have every opportunity to fulfill his or her dreams? And, what about their day-to-day care, security, and quality of life?

Let's put aside for a minute the technical reasons for planning. We will address them throughout this book. In your care, is a person you love dearly, and for whom you would do anything. There is no one who relies more on you than your child with special needs. You worry about him or her every day. Is she okay in school or at work? Are the teachers or co-workers treating her well? Did he take his medication properly and on time? Is she happy?

In addition to those concerns, bathing; dressing; toileting; feeding; transporting; monitoring medication; and going to therapies, are some of the many things you do daily. There is a lot to do isn't there? How in the world will anyone else know what, when, and how to do these things for your child if you don't put in writing this important information? Besides you who else can do this? Consider the adjustments you had to make in your life. This is important information that must be shared with current and future care providers. Let them learn from your experience.

What are your thoughts about putting money aside for your loved one's future? Where will he or she live? What about their education and, when possible, work? What people do you want in your child's life and what are their responsibilities? Have you discussed this subject with them? Have you asked them to serve as a Guardian or Trustee?

The point is that you have the answers, but they are worthless unless you put them in writing for current and future care providers. It will make the transition for your child and their care providers so much smoother and simpler after your death. Is it fair for the people you entrust with the care of your child to have to figure these things out as you did? You wouldn't leave your child for one day without giving detailed instructions. Yet, if you died today, you are leaving your child permanently, and then it is too late!

★ ★ ★

THE GOVERNMENT HAS A PLAN FOR YOU

THE GOOD NEWS: The Government Has a Plan for Your Child
THE BAD NEWS: The Government Has a Plan for Your Child

If you do not have a Will and Special Needs Trust, have done no Government Benefit planning, and have not identified the budgetary needs and the assets to fund it, there will be some very serious and detrimental consequences for your loved one and care providers.

The *good news* is that your state and federal government, knowing that very few families plan, has already prepared a plan for your child. The *bad news* is the plan itself. And this plan is in effect now and will begin tomorrow morning if you are no longer here.

Should you worry? See how your failure to take action automatically authorizes the state and/or federal government to take control of your estate and do the following:

— The State in which your loved one lives will choose the guardians, trustees and conservators. The Guardians will have the responsibility of day-to-day care. The Trustees will have control and authority over the distribution of any assets left to your child. Conservators manage your child's assets and their financial affairs.

— If the State is unable to find a single home for all your children, they could be forced to live in separate homes.

— Your estate will be distributed according to the rules of "Intestacy" in your State of residence. You have no say in this matter. If you are divorced from your child's biological parent and remarried, your current spouse receives all your personal property and can do anything they want with it. If you are unmarried, your children share your estate equally. Either way, your loved one with special needs may not get enough to live on or anything at all!

— Regardless of how much in assets your loved one receives in their name, this money is subject to immediate repayment to Medicaid for previously provided healthcare services.

— In addition to the payback to Medicaid, if the person's remaining assets exceed $2,000 they will be ineligible for SSI (Supplemental Security Income) and Medicaid. The result is the loss of part or all of their inheritance, ineligibility for SSI cash benefits and healthcare through Medicaid.

— Your child's standard of living could be seriously jeopardized with the loss of these benefits and assets. To make matters worse, there are no budgetary guidelines to know exactly what your child's monthly income requirements will be.

— Medicare may be the only healthcare benefit your child is eligible to receive. Your child will have to wait 25 months before their medical care is covered. Can your child afford to be without medical benefits for over two years? Your child will also lose valuable benefits such as prescription coverage under Medicare.

— The Government will also penalize your child if family and friends want to provide financial assistance. Gifts received by your child could be considered as income and/or assets. They will be used to "payback" Medicaid and, if they total over $2,000, they will cause the loss or reduction of SSI and Medicaid.

Two other very important issues are:

— Not all assets pass through a Will. Life insurance, retirement plans and annuities pass by beneficiary designation. Your child could receive these assets even if they are *not* named as a beneficiary. The result is the same, payback Medicaid and lose or reduce SSI.

— Without written information explaining the day-to-day care needs of your child and what your goals and wishes for their future care are, providers will only be able to do what they think you want, not necessarily what should be done.

When I share this information with families at conferences and workshops, their reactions are a mix of surprise, shock, fear and worry. You may be experiencing these same feelings. This is your child's plan for his or her lifetime, unless you take action now to change it! This book will show you how, what, when and where to take the proper steps to eliminate these problems and concerns. Wouldn't you agree that you should not be afraid of planning, but be afraid if you don't?

STORY 1 — *Divorce*

Marc and Amy divorced about 18 months after Kenny was born. The divorce wasn't pleasant, but it wasn't a war either. Marc agreed to Amy having custody of their two children. Kenny, who has Cornelia de Lange Syndrome, is the youngest.

Marc paid alimony and child support regularly for the first few months. His bi-monthly visits to the children became less and less frequent. Support checks arrived late and sometimes not at all. Marc remarried about two years later and moved to another state. The support checks stopped altogether as did the visits, the birthday, Christmas, Valentine and Easter cards and gifts. Amy was on her own.

Amy's family helped. Even Marc's parents provided some financial assistance. Amy inherited $300,000 from her grandfather. This was a tremendous help as it allowed her to work fewer hours at her job and spend more time with Kenny.

Kenny was 12 years old when Amy was diagnosed with breast cancer. Surgery and months of chemotherapy and radiation were unsuccessful. Believing she would not die, Amy did not make any provisions for her estate or children.

After Amy's death, Marc, being the biological father, was given custody of the children even with his history of defaulting on child support and not having seen the children in years. He also received control of Amy's estate.

Could this have been his motivation to get custody of the children? Control of their inheritance? Is Marc truly the person best suited to care for these children? Do you think this is what Amy wanted?

What could Amy have done to avoid this situation? There was no guarantee that Marc could be kept from getting custody of the children. Amy would have been wise to keep a journal of missed support checks, the infrequent calls and visits, and how Marc voluntarily estranged himself from the children. At least other family members would have had a strong case to contest Marc's appointment as guardian and trustee. However, Amy could have guaranteed that Marc would have no access to or control of the money she left her children. A Special Needs Trust for Kenny and a traditional trust for her other child, would have a Successor Trustee appointed by Amy to manage and control the funds for the benefit of the children and out of the hands of Marc. The Successor Trustee also has sole discretion in disbursements from the Special Needs Trust.

Amy might have been able to convince Marc to rescind his parental rights leaving her able to appoint a Successor Guardian of her own choice. Regardless, she should have discussed this with him. She could have stated what she wanted for Kenny and made the necessary arrangements while she was still able.

If Marc violated his duties as Trustee and misused the assets in the trusts he would have been liable for criminal charges. However, the likelihood of the money being replaced is zero to none.

A big problem was ignored. The opportunity to resolve it easily was gone. This is not an uncommon occurrence.

★ ★ ★

EXCUSES FAMILIES MAKE TO AVOID PLANNING
First Define The Obstacles, Then Remove Them

★ Feel the process is too emotional, confusing and overwhelming.

Of course it is. If you have no guidance or method to follow it is far too difficult. Subjects that must be addressed include: Wills, Special Needs Trusts, Guardians, Trustees, Social Security, Financial Needs, and Lifestyle. However, your child and his or her future care providers will suffer the consequences if nothing is done.

★ Do not have a step-by-step method to guide them from beginning to completion.

This book will outline a 10-Step Method for beginning and finishing your plan.

★ Can't find attorneys and financial advisors in whom they have confidence that they have the necessary qualifications and expertise.

How to find and choose an affordable qualified attorney and other advisors will be discussed in Chapter 6.

★ Do not have enough time to do all the research and preparation.

This book will identify the problems, provide solutions, and give you the method to resolve them. The research has been done for you.

★ Have concerns about legal fees and other costs.

I have had families tell me they have been quoted as much as $10,000 for a Special Needs Trust. You will learn where and how to have your trust and wills prepared at a cost within your budget.

★ Believe their child is too young.

There is no minimum or maximum age to plan. The ideal time is <u>now</u> regardless of the age, type of disability, or the needs of the person. The consequences of not planning described earlier applies to all persons with special needs regardless of type, degree, age, or abilities of the person.

★ Hope their loved one will be cured or entirely self-sufficient.

No one knows what the future will be. Advances in medical science and therapies have given realistic hope to many families. However, planning should be done now for the reasons stated. Your plan should be based on the needs of your child today. As he or she grows and matures, you will update your plan and change it according to your child's needs.

★ Waiting to see if they will need a Special Needs Trust.

If your child's needs today require a Special Needs Trust, then do it. Not sure, do it anyway. The trust can remain unfunded without assets. If it is not needed in the future, simply change your Will and beneficiaries to pass assets directly to your child or to a traditional trust. It is unwise to plan based on what you hope for in the future versus what your child needs today.

★ Estate is not large enough.

One of the biggest misconceptions about trusts is that they are only for the wealthy. Nothing could be further from the truth. The Special Needs Trust should be created if the person with special needs is inheriting as little as $2,000. Whether your estate is $10,000 or $10,000,000 the Special Needs Trust is a key part of planning and appropriate for families now whether or not you put assets in today.

★ Concerned about what happens to funds in the trust if they are not needed.

Many families do not create a Special Needs Trust and fund it because they are concerned about the status of the assets in the trust if their child does not need them. Let us suppose that this is the case. Your child no longer has a disability or they do, and are totally self-sufficient needing little or no assistance. Since your child is the sole beneficiary of the trust, he or she is the only person who can receive the benefit of its income and assets. The Trustee may provide money for the beneficiary to pay for college, provide a down payment for a house, or capital to start a business. These assets are there for your child whether or not they have a disability.

★ Many single parents are concerned that after they die, a surviving ex-spouse (the other biological parent) will have access to and be able to take the assets left in a Special Needs Trust established by the deceased parent.

*The parent or other family member who establishes a Special Needs Trust usually is the trustee during their lifetime. No one can touch the assets in the trust without the trustee's consent. The parent establishing the Special Needs Trust can and should appoint Successor Trustees to take over after the parent dies or is unable to perform the duties of trustee. The surviving ex-spouse has no access to or authority over the trust unless he or she is appointed a trustee. It is suggested that a single parent in this situation appoint more than one Successor Trustee to ensure that the trust remains out of the hands of the surviving ex-spouse in the future. The parent or family member establishing the Special Needs Trust may specifically direct in the document that the surviving ex-spouse may never be appointed trustee. If there are other children, who are currently under age 18, they may be named as future trustees when they attain a certain age, over 18, chosen by you. (See **Story 1** on page 5)*

HINT ⭐ 1

INSTRUCTING YOUR SUCCESSOR TRUSTEE ON HOW TO DISBURSE FUNDS FROM THE SPECIAL NEEDS TRUST TO AN EX-SPOUSE WHO SURVIVES YOU AS GUARDIAN

When the surviving ex-spouse parent, who is the Guardian of your child, requests money from the Special Needs Trust, it is important that your Successor Trustee makes sure the money is spent on your child's needs and is not used for other purposes. One option is for your Successor Trustee to provide the funds and require a receipt for all purchases. This could cause some difficulty between the other parent and Trustees in getting the receipts. A more efficient and safer method is illustrated in the following example. Suppose the child with special needs requires a new bed and television. The parent contacts the Successor Trustee and requests $2,000 to purchase these items. Instead of the Trustee writing a check to the parent, the Trustee could request a bill from the store where the items are being purchased. The Trustee writes the check directly to the store. The parent never has possession or control of the money. By having the Special Needs Trust purchase the items, the Trust is also the owner of the property.

★ ★ ★

EVEN IF YOU HAVE DONE SOME PLANNING, ASK YOURSELF THESE QUESTIONS
If you answer "No" to any of these questions, you should review your plan again.

★ Have you prepared Wills and a Special Needs Trust?

★ Does your Special Needs Trust allow you and others to make gifts or leave money to it during your lifetime or only after your death?

★ Does your current Will exclude your loved one by name?

★ Do you have a written plan to let others know what you want in the future?

★ Have you made arrangements for Successor Guardians, Trustees, and Conservators?

★ Does the primary or secondary beneficiaries in your IRA, 401(k), annuities, and/or life insurance include the person with special needs?

★ Did you know that even if your loved one is *not* named as a beneficiary, he or she could receive proceeds anyway?

★ Do you understand all of the government benefit programs that are available for basic care and supervision and made sure that your loved one will be eligible?

★ Have you set aside any funds so your loved one will have a comfortable lifestyle with security, care, and quality of life?

CHAPTER   TWO

Life Planning Needs

1. LIFETIME SUPERVISION AND CARE

A. Decide if Supervision and Care are necessary and appropriate

B. Establish the level of care required
(Skilled Nursing to Occasional Assistance)

C. Consider Positions of Authority for Providers

a. Legal Guardianship

b. Limited Guardianship

c. Conservatorship

d. Durable Legal & Medical Power of Attorney

e. Trustees

(See the Glossary of Estate Planning Terms on page 109)

2. MAINTAINING GOVERNMENT BENEFITS ELIGIBILITY

A. Stay updated on eligibility requirements to be sure your child is
in compliance for the various Social Security cash and healthcare
benefits. Check with both your current state and any other state
your child may live in after your death as they may differ.

B. A person may be eligible for SSI, SSA, Medicaid and Medicare at the same time.

3. PROVIDE FOR THE PERSON'S SUPPLEMENTAL NEEDS

A. Government entitlements are intended to provide the essentials including food, shelter and clothing.

B. Eligibility guidelines for Social Security forbids the duplication of these needs by others. Non-compliance could result in forfeiture or reduction of benefits and the payback for those previously received. (This could also include payback for overpayment of Social Security cash benefits).

4. ARRANGE MANAGEMENT OF ASSETS

A. Creating a Special Needs Trust and appointing Successor Trustees will protect the assets you leave for your loved one. It will also maintain eligibility and avoid termination or payback of government benefits during your loved one's lifetime.

5. PREPARE DIGNIFIED FINAL ARRANGEMENTS

A. If you have specific wishes regarding your's and your loved one's final arrangements, it should be stated in their plan. Your child could survive you by 30 years or more. Who will remember your wishes?

6. AVOID FAMILY CONFLICT

A. If you provide no instructions or information to the family members who will care for your loved one, the result will be many different opinions and ideas as to what they think you want, and what your child needs. It will also most likely result in arguments and delays. Differences may have to be resolved by the courts.

C H A P T E R   T H R E E

Key Planning Issues

LIFESTYLE - LEGAL - FINANCIAL NEEDS - GOVERNMENT ENTITLEMENTS

LIFESTYLE planning is where the family puts in writing their instructions for care and what they want for the future of their loved one. This information is recorded in a document called the Letter of Intent. Although not a legal document, it is as important as the Will and Special Needs Trust. Lifestyle issues require decisions regarding where the person will live, continued educational programs, employment, social activities, religious affiliation, medical care, behavior management, advocacy and/or guardianship, trustees, and final arrangements. In addition, detailed instructions are provided for assisting the person with the typical activities of daily living such as bathing; dressing; feeding; and toileting. Perhaps the person has a special way of communicating that only the immediate family knows and understands. It is important that this information be included. It is recommended that families make a video of the person performing these activities and/or receiving assistance. When recording bathing and toileting, you can respect your child's dignity by having them wear a bathing suit or shorts and a T-shirt. In addition, show the person in different social settings such as;

home, school, day care center, work, etc. Prior to providing details regarding the assistance your loved one requires, it is important to give others details about what your child can do for themself. Their self-esteem, ego, and personal satisfaction in accomplishing a task is important. Great care and attention should be given to this subject as it plays an important role in the person's peace of mind and well being.

Imagine how much easier and less stressful it will be for your child and his or her care providers if they have detailed instructions immediately available to them rather than having to figure things out on their own. What could take weeks or months to learn, could be accomplished in a few days or even hours. The ultimate goal is to make the transition from parental care to independent living, residency in a group home, or moving in with other family members, as easy and comfortable as possible for all bearing in mind the comfort and security of your child.

LEGAL planning enables the family to state their wishes as to the distribution of their assets and appoint Executors to settle their estate. In conjunction with this, a Special Needs Trust is usually established to provide professional money management, appoint successor trustees and guardians, maintain government benefits, and protect the assets left for the individual. It is important to note that not all assets pass by your Will. Life insurance, retirement plans, and annuities pass by beneficiary designation in the policies or plans. It is therefore important to check how each asset in your estate will be transferred after your death and to whom.

The Irrevocable Living Special Needs Trust is the most commonly used document to provide supplemental funds for the exclusive benefit of the person with special needs. When properly drafted, the assets are not considered in the name of the person, so they will not cause the loss of SSI and healthcare benefits. In addition, these funds are not exposed to repayment of Medicaid benefits during your child's lifetime. This Trust has proven invaluable to families regardless of the size of their estate or the amount of assets they are leaving for the person. This Trust enables you to appoint trustees to manage the funds in the future after your death, or the inability to perform this function.

FINANCIAL NEEDS planning determines the supplemental needs of the person. Government SSI (Supplemental Security Income) provides monthly cash benefits to pay for food, shelter and clothing. The assets put aside are used for the person with special needs, and supplements what the government does not provide. First, a monthly budget is established based on today's needs while projecting for the future. By using a reasonable rate of return on your investments, calculate how much money is needed to fund the trust. For example, if you need to provide an additional $1,000 per month and you project a 6 percent return on your money, it would require $200,000 for the trust. $200,000 at 6 percent interest equals $12,000 per year or $1,000 per month. The life expectancy of the person must be considered because inflation will have an effect on the plan. Once this is completed, the family then chooses the assets to be placed into the trust. This may include stocks, mutual funds, IRAs, 401(k)s, real estate, home, and life insurance. Professional management for investing the assets may be done by the Trustee or they may hire financial advisors.

GOVERNMENT ENTITLEMENTS are for many persons, the only or primary source of income and healthcare. The cash and healthcare benefits are received through SSI (Supplemental Security Income), SSA (Social Security Survivor/Retirement Benefit), SSDI (Social Security Disability Income), Medicaid, and/or Medicare. A basic understanding of federal and state entitlement programs is essential in order to be sure that your child gets all that they are eligible to receive. It is important to make sure that assets received from family members through gifts and inheritance, or a settlement from litigation, does not result in the ineligibility, reduction, and/or termination of government benefits or the government claiming reimbursement from assets received by the person for benefits previously received. This is accomplished by making provisions through legal documents, beneficiary changes, and notification to other family that the person with special needs should not be named as a direct beneficiary. In fact, the person with special needs should be specifically excluded by name in a Will and Living Revocable Family Trust. *(Note: This cannot be done in Louisiana which has a "forced heir" rule which* *states that you cannot disinherit a child. — See "**Hint 10**", page 48)* They are not disinherited or slighted in any way. The Special Needs Trust is named to receive the assets intended for your loved one in order to avoid the loss of benefits or having to payback the government.

It is evident that each of these issues is interrelated and requires that they be coordinated through the planning process. Those persons who provide advice in one particular area should know what other advisors are doing. This emphasizes the importance of an organized plan and open communication between your advisors.

The result of completing a comprehensive plan assures: lifetime supervision and care; maintaining government benefits; makes available supplementary funds to help ensure a comfortable lifestyle; provides management of funds; leaves instructions for dignified final arrangements; and avoids family conflict.

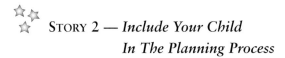

STORY 2 — *Include Your Child In The Planning Process*

One of the great rewards from my work is having the opportunity to meet many of the wonderful people who are a part of the special needs community. They include families, case workers, teachers, other professionals, and most importantly, the people with special needs.

Carol is one of the most memorable. She was 33 when she came to my office with her mother, Margaret. Carol was diagnosed with Autism at age four. Margaret told me that she was very delayed in walking, speaking, and doing most things for herself. She was told to put Carol in a "home" and let them take care of her. "No way," said Margaret. She worked and worked with Carol for years. The Carol I met, greeted me with a big hug and smile. I explained to Carol that the reason we were meeting was to discuss what her Mother and she wanted for the future. Carol sat down and began to tell me what she wanted. "Bart," she said, "I pay my own bills. I have a part-time job. I take the bus myself. I go to the mall and out at night with friends. And I want to have my own apartment and a full-time job!" Margaret's mouth dropped open. She was speechless. I loved it. Margaret turned to Carol and asked, "Why didn't you ever tell me this?" "Because you never asked," she responded.

Families make so many decisions for their young children with special needs that they forget that as they grow and mature, they may be very capable of making some decisions of their own. My approach to planning is to first focus on the person's abilities and then "fill in the gaps" where they need assistance.

Not only is it important to ask, it is just as important to let your loved one try different things. Our greatest lessons are learned in this way. Is there any reason why a person with special needs should not have the same opportunities as everyone else?

C H A P T E R   F O U R

Ten Simple Planning Steps

You can prepare a plan in a simple step-by-step method without feeling overwhelmed by the process if you follow these ten life planning steps. Suppose you had a party at your home last New Year's Eve. You woke up the next morning and the house was a mess. The living room, kitchen, den, bedrooms, bathrooms and even the patio needed a major cleanup. You could have done one of two things. You could ignore it, even though it would not go away. Or, you could work on one room at a time, and little by little it starts to come together. If you follow the steps in this chapter, you will create a plan that addresses the lifestyle and care needs of your child. Work on one step at a time and no more than an hour or two each day. By doing this, you will have time to review each step. You will have time to think about what you want and not feel pressured or overwhelmed. Within a few days your plan will come together and you will have it completed.

Step 1 — Decide What You Want For The Future
   A. Residential Needs
       a. Live independently with some assistance
       b. Reside in a Group Home

c. Live with family or friends

d. Skilled Nursing Facility with 24 hour care

Making arrangements for residential living is not only for after your death. Parents sometimes have to make decisions that are in the best interest of their child, but not necessarily what they ideally want. This may be one of them. The issue of a child moving out of the parents home can be very difficult. Your child's best interests should take priority.

H I N T

INDEPENDENT LIVING

If and when your child is old enough, and shows the potential ability to live independently away from your home, don't you think you owe them the chance to try? You may make a "trial run" by renting a furnished apartment near your home on a month-to-month lease or choose a nearby group home. See how things go. You are only a few minutes away if needed. If it does not work out, try something else.

If a group home or other facility is what your child needs, start to look now regardless of your child's age. First, decide in which community your child will live. If Uncle Bob and Aunt Linda will be the Guardians and live in another state, that is where you should look. Some subsidized group homes take 70 percent of your child's Social Security check as full room and board. Others can cost thousands of dollars each month. It is up to you to decide what fits your child's budget and needs.

If your child will be living with relatives, will any adjustments be needed to the home to accommodate your loved one? Does it need to be wheelchair accessible? Should another room be added? What about a special shower, lower kitchen counters, and raised electrical outlets? These are just some of the considerations for making your loved one's residence as accessible, functional, and comfortable as possible. These modifications can be budgeted for now and the funds provided through the Special Needs Trust to be used

---

HINT

FINDING A GROUP HOME

Make a list of group homes. Visit and tour them. If they are near where the future guardians live, have them make the visit and inspection. Get details on current costs and projected increases. If necessary, get on the waiting list now of each group home you like. If there is an opening before your child is ready, you can always pass until you are ready.

---

when needed. Check with local government agencies to see if there are subsidies available. Are there local contractors experienced in this type of work? Is any of this work tax deductible?

B. Employment

Provide information on any and all past work experience. Describe what your child's duties were at work and any special arrangements that need to be made. Request letters of recommendation from employers and others. Identify businesses who hire people with special needs. Ask if there are employment opportunities for your child.

HINT **4**

LIVING IN THE FAMILY HOME

Many families would like their child to remain in the family home after the parents die. A person on SSI and Medicaid may own the home they live in personally, although this is not always best. If rooms are rented to others, it may result in personal income to your child that could effectively reduce or terminate SSI cash benefits and Medicaid. Another option is to leave the home to the Special Needs Trust. The Trustee collects any rent from other tenants on behalf of the Special Needs Trust and can use this rental income as supplemental funds to support their loved one.

☆☆☆ STORY 3 — *The Pizza Man*

Self-esteem, security and quality of life are critical issues in all our lives. It is no different for people with special needs. It becomes even more important at the time of transition when a parent dies. Planning to make sure this period is as easy as possible can affect the person for life.

When Della came to see me she was 77 years old. Widowed many years before, she lived in a retirement community in Arizona with her son, Wayne, who was 43 and has mild mental retardation. Della and I had several meetings. Each time Wayne would come dressed in his work uniform cap and shirt. He works for one of the national pizza companies. I would kid him about always coming to the office in his uniform, without a pizza. He would smile and say, "Next time." Wayne loves his job. The first part of each of our meetings was spent with Wayne telling me about his day at work.

Della's plans were to have Wayne live with his brother, Larry, in Philadelphia after her death. "I hope he will be able to find the same job there," she said. "He so looks forward to work and seeing his friends there. Everyone loves him. I hate to think of him not being able to continue." I suggested that Della call Larry and ask him to contact the pizza franchise in his neighborhood and to ask about them hiring Wayne in the future even though we had no idea when this would happen. Della loved the idea and said she would do it. She called me a few days later and told me that Larry went to the pizza place. The manager said that Wayne had a job waiting whenever he is ready.

Della, of course, was delighted. By taking a few minutes to do this, Larry took a major step in giving his Mom peace of mind about Wayne's job, but more importantly, this will make Wayne's transition after his Mother's death and having to leave his home in Arizona much easier. Each pizza franchise store is built identically. Wayne could walk into a restaurant in Phoenix, Philadelphia, Beijing or London and they are all the same. Wayne will be able to have something familiar waiting for him when he leaves for his new home with Larry.

C. Education

Children with special needs may stay in the public school system until age 22. The quality of programs and services varies greatly between cities, counties and states. Find out what educational programs are available if your child will be moving to another community after your death. Retain copies of their records including IEPs (Individual Educational Profile). Provide information on what you want for your child after public school such as continuing educational programs and job training.

H I N T

THE IEP (INDIVIDUAL EDUCATION PROFILE)

If your child is in public school, then you have probably experienced an IEP meeting. States differ in their policies regarding the participation of interested parties (parents, guardians, case workers, etc.) in the IEP meeting, when the person with special needs reaches age 18, "the age of majority." It may not be possible to participate in the IEP meeting without complying with certain requirements set forth by each state. For example, in Arizona, if the person with special needs is over age 18 the only person(s) who can attend the IEP meeting are the legal guardians. If the person does not have a legal guardian, they can sign an IEP Power of Attorney and authorize whomever they want to attend the IEP meeting and act in their behalf. While your child is under age 22 and attending public school, make sure you check with the school districts where you currently live and the one where your child will live after your death, to learn what their requirements are for current and future care providers to be able to attend the IEP meeting.

D. Social Activities

Make a list of all the activities your loved one enjoys. Include the type of activity; when and where it is held; how your child participates; who conducts the activity; and the cost. There may be things your child wants to do that are inappropriate for them. Be sure to list these as well. Information on activities is typically available through local organizations and support groups.

E. Medical Records

1. Maintain up-to-date medical information.
2. Keep a list of names, addresses and phone numbers for current and previous medical practitioners.
3. Include items like: Diagnoses; Functioning; Vision; Hearing; Speech; Mobility; Nursing Needs; Therapy; Allergies; and Prescription and Over-the-Counter Medications (what worked and what did not).

An example of a very important piece of information relates to one of my clients, Stewart, who has Prader-Willi Syndrome. He is also non-verbal. This is a condition that involves uncontrolled eating. His family must lock the refrigerator and food cupboard. Regardless, he is able to get food which results in frequent belly aches. Here is the key information. Stewart will only take one particular brand of antacid when he is ill. Suppose you are taking care of Stewart and he gets one of his severe belly aches. He is not able to tell you what he wants. Maybe you have another brand which he will not take. You try to give it to Stewart but he spits it out. You throw your hands up in frustration because you don't want him to suffer, but you don't know what to do. If only his parents had left written instructions that wherever Stewart is, make sure there is his brand of antacid immediately available. I bet you can think of similar things like this that relate to your child.

Another example of wise planning is the following. Suppose your child will not or is not able to sit still in the dentist's chair. You may be using a dentist who has an anesthesiologist available to assist in sedating patients for treatment. You would certainly want to make sure that future care providers know about this and have found a dentist in their community who works with an anesthesiologist and can provide the same service.

F. Dietary Needs

Make a list of:

1. Required foods for breakfast, lunch, dinner and snacks;
2. Restricted foods;
3. Food preferences;
4. Food allergies.

G. General Lifestyle - Daily Living Skills, Abilities, & Behavior

Include details about anything and everything you want people to know about your child. If you are not sure, include it. It is important to be sensitive to how your child may interpret actions by others. A simple act could send a message that is completely different than what is intended. An example where this could happen, might be as simple as a visiting relative seeing your child in the kitchen making a peanut butter and jelly sandwich. The relative wants to be nice and takes the knife from your child and makes the sandwich out of pure love. Where your typical child would love being spoiled, the message to your child with special needs may be, "you are not capable of doing this." Let others know that they should be aware of not only what they do, but how they do it and the effect it will have on your child.

Your child's speech may be difficult to understand, or you may have a special way of communicating that only the immediate family knows. For example, an expression or body position might indicate to you that your child is hungry or needs to use the bathroom. Putting this on video and explaining the various signs or what the person is saying is critically important.

STORY 4 — *Bubba, Bubba, Bubba*

Michael is 42 years old and lives with his mother, Anne. Michael has multiple disabilities. His communication and functioning skills are at the level of a two year old. He uses a wheelchair and requires assistance for all his needs. Anne has cared for him his entire life.

Michael is able to speak a few words. One of the things he does is roll his head from side to side, smile and say, "Bubba, Bubba, Bubba." I asked Anne what Michael meant. "What do you think it means?" she responded. I told her I had no idea. Anne said, "Bubba, Bubba, Bubba means bubbles!" So I assumed Michael wanted Anne to blow bubbles for him. Anne further explained, "It's the bubbles in a soft drink. He likes the tickle in his throat when he drinks it."

It is a cute story, however, it made me think. Anne had done no planning. There was no written information or instructions for Michael's care needs. Imagine if Michael came to live with you and you have to figure everything out yourself. You watch him roll his head and hear Michael say, "Bubba, Bubba, Bubba" a few times each day. What would you think he meant? After a few days he says it again, this time without a smile and fewer times each day. By the end of two weeks he never says it again.

Michael's limited communication skills allowed him to express a desire for one of the few things that made him happy and gave him pleasure. Who knows what self-esteem he felt because he was able to make a request and have it understood and fulfilled. What a tragedy it would be if Anne died and never let anyone know about, "Bubba, Bubba, Bubba." Think about how well and secure Michael would feel, if after losing his Mother, being moved from his home, and changing his life completely, he says to his new care providers, "Bubba, Bubba, Bubba," and they know to give him that favorite soft drink. How do you think it would make Anne feel if she could see Michael's smile?

STEP 2 — THE LETTER OF INTENT

Informational & Lifestyle Instructions

Put your hopes, desires, instructions, and goals for your loved one in a written **Letter of Intent.** This is not a legal document. There is no need to be concerned about it complying with laws or regulations. Include information regarding care providers and assistance, attending physicians, dentists, medicine, functioning abilities, types of activities enjoyed, daily living skills, diet, monitoring medication, and rights and values. Make a video of people interacting with your loved one at home, school, work, communicating and assisting with daily activities and needs. All the information compiled in *Step 1* should be included in this document.

This is a document that will be continually updated. As your child grows and changes so will his or her needs and abilities. A great way to remember to update the Letter of Intent is to make the review a birthday present each year.

After you complete the Letter of Intent, give a copy to everyone who provides services to, or for, your child. Not only to inform them, but to also give them an opportunity to provide feedback on what they know about your child that can also be added. Make sure future Guardians, Trustees, and Conservators have copies now. By doing so, they can ask questions while you are here to provide information.

Maintaining your Letter of Intent on your computer provides an easy way to update it on a regular basis and share it with others.

The Letter of Intent is a document that can play an important part in your loved one's life today. As new people become active in your child's life (teacher, therapist, case worker, etc.) the Letter of Intent will assist them in getting to know your child better and faster. Suppose you receive a call from a new case worker assigned to your child. This happens all to frequently. You arrange a meeting that you have done many times already. As much as you love your child, it gets to be a bit of a nuisance to have to explain and show the new case worker all they need to know about your child. Give the new case worker a copy of the Letter of Intent and video to review prior to their visit. In this way, they have all the information they will need and it will take them a fraction of the time to learn about your child. In addition, if they have questions, they can first refer to your letter. Do the same with new doctors, new teachers, new employers, etc.

STEP 3 — GUARDIANSHIP & CONSERVATORSHIP

H I N T

REMEMBERING
ITEMS FOR THE
LETTER OF INTENT

When you think of an item to put in the Letter of Intent while at work, in your car, or any other activity, call your home and leave the information on your answering machine. If near a computer, send an e-mail. Getting home after a long day, you may forget what you wanted to put in the letter. This is a great reminder.

Many parents of persons with special needs think they continue to have the same authority on behalf of their loved one after they reach age 18 because of the disability. This is not the case. Every American citizen is an "Emancipated Adult" when they reach the age of majority at 18. This results in parents no longer having the authority to make medical and legal decisions on behalf of their child.

Guardianship and Conservatorship (see *Glossary of Estate Planning Terms* on page 109) are legal appointments requiring court ordered mandates. Individuals or institutions manage the estate of people judged incapable (not necessarily incompetent) of managing their own personal affairs. Guardians and conservators are also responsible for the care and decisions made on behalf of people who are unable to care for themselves. You should first ask yourself and decide if legal guardianship is necessary and appropriate. Legal guardianship may not be appropriate for the person if they are able to perform most tasks for themselves, are gainfully employed, and are living, to some degree, independently. Knowing the needs of your loved one will be a major factor in making this decision. Legal counsel, care providers, and physicians should be consulted for guidance. An alternative to guardianship would be a Durable Legal and Medical Power of Attorney. The person with special needs must be able to understand and sign a legal document. This would provide others with the authority to make legal and medical decisions on behalf of the person, if and when they are unable. When the person with special needs gives their "Power of Attorney," they have the option to cancel it at any time.

A decision needs to be made as to whether you will elect full legal guardianship, limited guardianship or none at all. Laws governing Guardianship vary between states. Organizations like The Arc (See **Resource Information**, page 100) provide excellent information on this subject. Consulting with an attorney who specializes in guardianship is also suggested. If you decide that legal guardianship is not necessary, it is recommended that you still make provisions for guardianship in your Wills and/or Trusts should it become necessary later in your loved one's life.

Next, make a list of anyone you feel is a good candidate to fill either or both positions. This can be relatives, friends, private fiduciaries, or agencies. Review your list and decide in what order you would want these people to serve as your Successor Guardians and/or Trustees when you are no longer able. Discuss your wishes with each person and let them decide. You may have other children whom you would like to name; however, they may be minors (under age 18) who cannot serve. You could name minor children to serve in the future when they reach a certain age that you select. The minimum age is 18. You are not obligated to appoint the spouse of anyone you name as a Guardian or Trustee. You may have more than one serve at a time as a Co-Guardian and/or Co-Trustee. Your child could survive every Guardian you appoint. You may add a provision stating that the "last surviving Guardian shall have the right to appoint his or her successor(s)." By the way, when possible, ask your child who he or she would like to have as a guardian in the future if you are not here.

The Special Needs Trust, although irrevocable, may allow you to add, delete, or change the order of Guardians and Trustees. Do not do this without the assistance of an attorney.

Since most people who agree to be Guardians and/or Trustees are not fully aware of their responsibilities, it is suggested that you provide them with this information. As these positions differ between states, you should obtain information from each appropriate one.

Give copies of the *Letter of Intent*, when completed, to the named Guardians and Trustees. Have the Successor Guardians spend time with your loved one in order to familiarize themselves with providing hands-on care while you are here to instruct, guide and answer questions. When the Successor Guardians feel comfortable and competent to care for your loved one, have them spend time alone with them for a weekend or longer. This will also give you an opportunity for some free time to yourself and maybe even get away for a weekend!

If you have no family or friends to fulfill these important roles, consider private fiduciaries or better yet, speak with other families in your local support groups who are in the same situation. You might want to consider an arrangement where you agree with another family to care for each other's children if it becomes necessary.

☆☆
☆ STORY 5 — *Guardianship: Don't Be Afraid To Ask*

Ruth lives in Flagstaff, Arizona with her daughter, Melissa. Ruth is 52 years old and widowed. She sells real estate which provides a modest living, yet gives her great flexibility in being able to adjust her schedule in order to be with Melissa at any time. Melissa is 23 years old and has Cerebral Palsy. She is non-verbal, has severe mental retardation and uses a wheelchair. Melissa lives at home with Ruth. Daily respite care assistance is provided through state programs in Arizona. Melissa requires skilled 24 hour care.

Ruth asked me to assist her in preparing a Special Needs Plan for Melissa. During our discussion, I asked Ruth who she would like to appoint as the Guardians for Melissa to succeed her after her death or inability to serve. Ruth became quite emotional and said the only family she had was her sister and brother-in-law. She knew they would be terrific Guardians for Melissa, however, she was reluctant to ask. Ruth further explained to me that her sister and brother-in-law could not be the Guardians because they did not have a lot of money to support their own children, let alone Melissa. She said she felt uncomfortable "putting them on the spot" asking for their help. I explained to Ruth that money should not be a factor in this issue of Guardianship because we already established that between government healthcare benefits, Social Security, and the assets she left in the Special Needs Trust, there would be more than enough funds to pay for the necessary services.

It was obvious to me, and I am sure to you by now, Ruth was simply afraid to ask. Sitting at her kitchen table, wiping her tears, I asked, "What other decisions have you made for your sister and her family that she doesn't know about?" "What do you mean?" asked Ruth. "Well, you have decided for your sister and brother-in-law, and Melissa as well, that they cannot be her future Guardians. Furthermore, Melissa is unable to ask her Aunt and Uncle and is depending on you to do that for her. If the answer, is 'no,' we'll work together to figure something out." Ruth promised to ask.

Back at my office in Phoenix a few days later, the phone rang and it was a very emotional Ruth. She said, "Bart, I called my sister and brother-in-law and asked if they would be Melissa's Successor Guardians. Without a pause they said, "Yes, we've been waiting for you to ask!""

So, don't keep anyone waiting. Don't make assumptions. Ask now and get them prepared.

STEP 4 — DETERMINE THE COST OF YOUR PLAN

Make a list of current and anticipated monthly expenses. It should be simple to list itemized expenses (food, shelter, clothing, cable TV, telephone, ride to work, social activities, personal hygiene items, therapy, dentist, etc.) for an adult. For a small child you may just want to select an amount that you feel is adequate. It could be $500 or $5,000. When this amount has been established, decide on a reasonable interest rate of return and estimate how much you will need to put in the trust in order to provide enough funds to support your loved one's lifestyle. Government cash benefits will offset the amount needed. The effects of inflation should also be considered based on your child's life expectancy.

It is suggested that you increase the budget by at least 10 percent to give you a hedge against any unforeseen expenses. Better to have more than to fall short.

Inflation will affect your plan in the future. If you had $100,000 in a trust today, in just ten short years at 3 percent inflation, the buying power is reduced to $74,000! That's a 26 percent loss. This does not mean that if the trust needs $750,000 40 years from now, you need to come up with this money now. However, it would be wise to overfund the Special Needs Trust at your death in order to allow for principal growth to combat the effects of inflation. Of course you should review the budgetary needs at least once a year and make any necessary changes. If money is left to the Trust by others, this can also be used as an offset.

STEP 5 — IDENTIFY RESOURCES TO FUND YOUR PLAN

Resources that may be used to provide income include government benefits, family assistance, inheritance, savings, life insurance, pensions, real estate, and investments. Most families do not have the available assets to fund the Trust immediately, but designate specific assets through their Wills and beneficiary designations on insurance and retirement plans.

<u>*Do not deposit any Social Security cash benefits, checks made payable to your child or any assets belonging to your child directly into a Special Needs Trust that was established prior to January 1, 2000*</u>.

H I N T

DON'T RELY ON OTHERS GOOD INTENTIONS

Do not count on any gifts until they are actually in the trust. People and their circumstances change. There is no guarantee that promised money will ever make it into the Special Needs Trust. Make it your responsibility to fully fund the needs of the trust. You can always adjust these numbers as assets are received from others in the future.

(See Chapter 5, *Social Security Government Benefit Entitlements)* for details on how to transfer these funds into the Special Needs Trust.

Family and friends may tell you that they are leaving assets for the care of your child. It is imperative that they do it in the right way. Leave it to the Special Needs Trust, *not* in your child's name.

H I N T ⭐**8**

WHEN TO NAME THE SPECIAL NEEDS TRUST AS BENEFICIARY

If your life insurance and pension plan are going to be needed for your spouse and all children, do not leave any of these assets to the Special Needs Trust. Assets in a Special Needs Trust can only be used for the person with special needs. Your spouse will provide anything your children need. Therefore, leave it to your surviving spouse or a family trust. Make sure that your child with special needs is not named as a beneficiary of the Family Trust. At your spouse's subsequent death, his or her Will (or the Family Trust) will state which assets go into the Special Needs Trust. The Second or Contingent Beneficiary, named in your life insurance, pensions and annuities, can be the Special Needs Trust. Do not leave any assets by beneficiary designation to the Special Needs Trust until after it has been signed and notarized. You can sign your Wills and execute the Trust at the same time.

STEP 6 — PREPARE LEGAL DOCUMENTS

One of the biggest obstacles to planning and most common reasons families give for not preparing a plan for the future care of their loved one is because they cannot find an attorney who either knows anything about this planning, or is qualified to draft a Special Needs Trust. Most attorneys know little or nothing about this subject. This is due to the fact that few attorneys have been approached to do this work and; consequently, don't pursue it. Paying an attorney "to learn" by having him or her research how to prepare the Special Needs Trust can be costly to you. Fees can reach up to $10,000. Organizations and support agencies may be able to refer you to experienced attorneys. Typical fees for the Special Needs Trust range from $500 to $1,500.

Before we discuss the Special Needs Trust, I want to emphasize how important it is to include other family members in the planning process. Especially the Grandparents. Whether family members intend to leave assets to your child with special needs or nothing at all, their actions or inaction could have severe consequences. The following Stories and Hint will illustrate these circumstances and tell you how to prevent them from happening to your child.

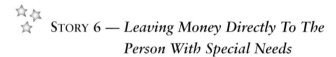

STORY 6 — *Leaving Money Directly To The Person With Special Needs*

Jimmy's grandparents decided to leave $100,000 for his lifetime care after their death. They met with their attorney who drafted their Wills. They never mentioned to the attorney that Jimmy has Autism and that he receives SSI and Medicaid. Unfortunately, the attorney never asked the purpose of the trust. Jimmy was nine years old at the time his grandparents made these arrangements.

Grandma died a few years later. When Jimmy was 31, Grandpa passed away. Jimmy's Dad was the Executor of Grandpa's estate. He was thrilled to learn, for the first time, that Jimmy was to receive $100,000 from Grandpa's estate directly in his name.

Neither Jimmy's parents or grandparents did any special needs planning. As Jimmy's Representative Payee, his Mother received his SSI checks. Each year she filed a required report to SSI on how she used the money. She answered a question on the form stating that Jimmy had received $100,000 from his grandparents. A few weeks after sending her annual report, she received notification that Jimmy was now ineligible for SSI and Medicaid. His benefits were to be terminated. She was also notified that Jimmy had been on Medicaid since he was 18 years old and in those 13 years he had been provided with $43,000 in medical aid. Jimmy's Mom was instructed to send a check from his inheritance for repayment in the amount of $43,000.

Grandma and Grandpa's well-meaning generosity resulted in chaos. Almost half the money was taken by Medicaid. Jimmy lost his monthly cash income of SSI and no longer had any Medicaid coverage. When Jimmy's Mom called Social Security and asked what she had to do in order to reinstate his benefits, she was told to "spend down" the remaining $57,000 until it was below $2,000. This situation happens all the time. What is so sad is that it could have been easily avoided.

Had Mom and Dad prepared a plan including an Irrevocable Living Special Needs Trust, the Grandparents could have left the $100,000 to the Trust instead of one in Jimmy's name. The result would be no payback to Medicaid and continued eligibility for SSI and Medicaid during Jimmy's lifetime. In addition, Jimmy would have been able to benefit from the entire $100,000 inheritance instead of the government taking almost half. If the Special Needs Trust were created prior to January 1, 2000, there would be no payback to Medicaid for medical assistance. (See Step 7, page 44 Special Needs Trusts Established After January 1, 2000 and page 47, Special Needs Trusts Established Before January 1, 2000).

 STORY 7 — *Leaving Assets Intended For Your Loved One To Your Other Children*

Marshall and Emily were sure they had done their planning correctly. In their Wills they left nothing to their son, Eddie, who has multiple disabilities. The plan was to leave everything in their estates to their two daughters and not create a Special Needs Trust. They even had the foresight to specifically state that Eddie was to receive nothing. They made the necessary beneficiary changes in their life insurance and pension plans.

"We don't think we need any of your services," Emily told me, "however, we thought it would be a good idea to check." I congratulated both Emily and Marshall for the work they had already done. There was nothing wrong with their plan. However, there did exist some issues that could have a devastating effect on Eddie's future financial security.

Emily told me that her daughters were married, had children, lived in Arizona, and had no Wills of their own. I explained to Emily and Marshall that the money they left to their daughters was legally theirs to do with as they wished and they were only under a moral obligation, not a legal obligation, to provide for Eddie. Emily told me that they trusted both girls implicitly and were okay with this arrangement.

"That's fine," I said. "Since the girls do not have Wills, their assets will pass to their husbands, if living, or their children after their deaths. The daughters' survivors also will have no legal obligation to provide for Eddie. Secondly, if your daughters or their husbands should have credit problems, litigation, health problems not covered by insurance or tax issues, the money intended for Eddie is liable to be used to satisfy these debts. There is no real guarantee that these assets will be safe from these contingencies. Another thing, money given to Eddie or used to provide for his necessities could result in loss of benefits or repayment of government benefits Eddie was not otherwise eligible to receive."

By now Emily and Marshall weren't looking as happy and confident as when they first walked into my office. I explained that there was a simple solution to this problem. Create a Special Needs Trust and leave assets intended for Eddie's care to the Trust. Next, name their daughters as Successor Co-Trustees after their death. I explained that it was also their decision as to whether or not they wanted their sons-in-law to be Co-Trustees with their wives. Regardless of what happens in their lives, the money in the Trust is safe. I further explained how they could appoint future Successor Trustees to follow their daughters.

Emily and Marshall were on the right track. Everything they did was correct, but it was not the best way to do things. We were able to "patch the holes in their plan" that would avoid the loss of any assets intended for Eddie's use.

Transferring Assets After The Death Of Relatives

The previous stories illustrate what happens when assets are passed directly to a loved one with special needs or another family member. There are other ways in which your loved one could receive assets directly **even if they are not specifically named.**

EXAMPLE A:
Grandparents Will Assets Directly To All Grandchildren

If Grandparents leave any assets through their Wills and Living Family Trusts "to all surviving grandchildren in equal shares" this will automatically include an equal share to the grandchild with special needs. Their Wills should specifically exclude the grandchild by name. "We leave nothing to our grandson, Robert Jones." Robert is **not being disinherited or slighted.** The Wills or Trust documents should say that the percentage designated for Robert Jones "shall go to The Robert Jones Special Needs Trust, dated September 1, 2002."

EXAMPLE B:
Grandparents Leave Assets To All Their Children Per Stirpes

Assume that Robert's mother, Mary, is one of three children. Her parents state in their Wills that they leave their assets "to all of their surviving children in equal shares per stirpes." Per Stirpes means that if a parent leaves property to each child and one of them dies before one or both parents, then the deceased child's portion will pass on to their surviving children. The result would be that Robert would receive all or a portion of Mary's share directly in his name.

To avoid this from happening, the Grandparents should state that if Mary does not survive them, her portion or a percentage of it goes to "The Robert Jones Special Needs Trust, dated September 1, 2002." Again they should state in their Wills and/or Trusts that Robert Jones receives nothing directly. If Robert has siblings, they could receive their portion directly.

EXAMPLE C:

Grandparents Leave Assets To All Their Children Per Capita

Take the same situation illustrated in Example B except the Wills and Trusts leave their assets "to all of their surviving children in equal shares per capita." Per Capita means that if a parent leaves property to each child and one of them dies before one or both parents, then the deceased child's portion will pass on to their siblings, **not their surviving children.** If Mary dies before her parents, her brothers and sisters share her portion of the estate. Robert and/or his Special Needs Trust and his siblings receive nothing.

If this is not what the Grandparents want, they should consult with legal counsel to add a codicil (amendment) to their Wills and Trusts and change the distribution to "per stirpes."

EXAMPLE D:

Grandparents Want Their Own Trust And Trustees

The Grandparents may not want your spouse, their son-in-law or daughter-in-law, as a Co-Trustee having authority over the assets they leave for your child with special needs. Or, they may wish to decide who gets the remainder of their assets left in the Special Needs Trust after your child's death. If either of these situations or a different one exists, Grandparents can create their own Special Needs Trust. They can then appoint anyone they want as Trustees and Successor Trustees. They can also stipulate who gets the remainder of the trust after your child dies. Your child can have more than one Special Needs Trust created for them. Both sets of Grandparents may have differing wishes resulting in three trusts.

EXAMPLE E:

Bequests From Aunts & Uncles

Any family or friends whom you think might leave something to your child should be informed on how to leave it to the Special Needs Trust. Suppose you have a brother who is not married and has no children. If he has no Will, his estate will go to your parents if they are living, at his death. If not, his estate passes to his surviving siblings. If you are his only sibling and don't survive your brother, guess who gets his estate? That's right, your child!

This is not the time to be hesitant to speak with your family members. Think how upset they would be if it was too late and you never told them how to properly pass assets to your child with special needs.

EXAMPLE F:
Not All Property Passes Through Your Will Or Living Family Trust

Typically, only your personal property is passed through your Will. Your assets may be placed in a Living Revocable Family Trust, however, these assets are still yours. Life insurance, annuities, and pension plans (401(k)s, IRAs, etc.) pass by beneficiary designation. If you have a Living Revocable Family Trust, you may have named it as the beneficiary of these policies. Once the proceeds from these assets are paid to the trust, they are distributed according to the guidelines of the trust.

In most families, the spouse is named as the First or Primary Beneficiary. Let us assume that Dad has a life insurance policy and IRA with Mom as the First Beneficiary. If Mom dies before Dad and then Dad dies, the death benefit is paid to the Second or Contingent Beneficiary. Unless Dad states a beneficiary other than the child with special needs, that child will receive all or an equal portion with his or her siblings. If Dad designates no Second Beneficiary, it automatically goes to all surviving children in equal shares. Again, any portion of these items intended for your child should specifically name their Special Needs Trust as the recipient.

Here is the *bottom line* about everything that you just read. Identify and address the various ways in which your child could possibly receive money, assets, gifts, etc. Then make sure that the *way* is blocked by redirecting the items to the Special Needs Trust.

HINT ⭐**9**

MAKE SURE OTHER FAMILY MEMBERS' DOCUMENTS ARE CORRECT

I have been assisting and educating families on how to plan since 1993. I have met with a few stubborn family members who think that no one can tell them anything. After one grandmother described to me what clearly was not a Special Needs Trust, I suggested she have it reviewed. "Well," she said in a huff, "my son-in-law is one of the top CPAs in our state. He knows what he is doing." I said, "For your grandson's benefit, wouldn't you want to be absolutely sure?" Just because someone has impressive credentials in accounting, law, or financial planning, it does not mean that they have any knowledge about special needs planning.

About three weeks later I received a call from the Grandmother's daughter. They had the documents reviewed and it was confirmed that the "Special Needs Trust" the Grandmother thought she had was indeed a Living Revocable Family Trust without any special needs provisions. Her grandson was also named as a direct recipient of assets.

STEP 7 — CONSIDER CREATING A SPECIAL NEEDS TRUST

The key to creating a proper Special Needs Trust is that it must be in compliance with government regulations. This means that it must have the approval of both Social Security and Medicaid. In either case, the person may lose the benefits of the trust and/or may lose their government benefits until all of the money in the trust is gone.

The Special Needs Trust holds assets for the benefit of persons with special needs and uses the income to provide for their supplemental needs. When drafted properly, assets are not considered in the person's name so as not to jeopardize government entitlements including cash and healthcare benefits. It can avoid or defer repayment of healthcare provided by Medicaid. This depends on when the Special Needs Trust was established. (See Step 7, page 44 *Special Needs Trusts Established After January 1, 2000* and page 47, *Special Needs Trusts Established Before January 1, 2000).* Trustees are appointed to manage the trust and successor trustees are also named to take over at the trustee's death or inability to serve.

The Special Needs Trust is not designed to save your family any estate taxes, nor will the use of a Will and Special Needs Trust avoid probate. If you want to avoid probate, which may result in delays in the distribution of your estate when you die (and can cost your heirs 10 percent of the estate, even if it is a simple one under $100,000), you will need to see an attorney to help you in creating a Living Family Revocable Trust. This is a legal document that is used in traditional estate planning.

If you are not sure, arrange an initial consultation with an attorney. Many offer free initial consultations. Regardless, the cost could result in dramatic savings in your estate taxes. New tax laws pertaining to estates, recently enacted, make this even more timely and important.

The Special Needs Trust is not a difficult trust to create. It will work in almost all situations and will be the safest in protecting your loved one's assets and benefits. Although the Trust could be revocable and still conform to the law, sometimes families have had difficulties with Social Security when they have a Revocable Special Needs Trust. The Social Security rules about revocability of the trust are technical. They can be confusing, even amongst attorneys, as to what they mean. To be safe, discuss with your attorney making the Special Needs Trust irrevocable.

Even though it is irrevocable, you may be able to change the persons you have appointed as Trustees, the persons you have appointed as your loved one's Personal Representative (Guardian), and who or what will receive the Trust assets when your loved one dies. You can even make substantial amendments to the Trust if the law changes so that the Trust, as written, will carry out your wishes. These options will be affected by how the trust was originally drafted and the state in which you reside. Do not attempt to make changes without the assistance of an attorney. Make sure you have both Social Security and Medicaid check the documents for compliance. There is a specific procedure to follow in order to have your Special Needs Trust reviewed. Turn to page 48 ("**Hint 10**" - **Planning, Signing, Checking for Compliance**) for instructions. It may be necessary to establish an entirely new Special Needs Trust.

Key Points Of The Special Needs Trust

A. The Trust is not in the person's name although they are listed as the sole beneficiary of the Trust.

B. Assets and income from the Trust may only be used to provide for the supplemental needs of the named person (beneficiary). They may not duplicate the intended benefits of SSI which includes food, shelter, and clothing.

C. Assets in the Trust do not belong to the named beneficiary (person with special needs).

D. The Trustee(s) have the sole discretion in distributing the assets and income from the Trust. No one else has access or authority over the trust. Ex-spouses and other family members providing care and supervision must request any needed trust income or assets from the Trustee. The Trustee makes the decision.

E. Depending on the type of Special Needs Trust you create and the date it was established, several things can happen when the beneficiary (person with special needs) dies. The remainder of the trust can be distributed to you, your designated "Remaindermen," or may be required to payback Medicaid.

Special Needs Trusts Established After January 1, 2000

The majority of those who read this book have not yet established a Special Needs Trust. The following information pertains to new Special Needs Trusts established after January 1, 2000. Those of you who already have a trust may have concerns regarding it being in compliance. Trusts established prior to January 1, 2000 will be discussed in this chapter.

The new requirement for Special Needs Trusts established *after* January 1, 2000 is the inclusion of a clause that provides for Medicaid to be the first recipient of the remainder of the trust as a payback for services. Any assets remaining after Medicaid is satisfied, are disbursed to the remaindermen named in the Special Needs Trust. If the payback amount to Medicaid exceeds the amount of assets in the Special Needs Trust, no other family members are liable to satisfy the payback out of their own assets.

The following sample payback provision wording for Special Needs Trusts that are dated after January 1, 2000 is taken directly from Social Security's website. The information can be found under the following title: SI 01120.201 *Exceptions to Counting Trusts Established on or after 1/1/00.* This is an example only. Although this example is in compliance with Social Security, it may not be in compliance for Medicaid in your state. Each state may require different wording. This should be confirmed when you follow the instructions in **"Hint 10"** on checking for compliance from Social Security and Medicaid.

The State will receive all amounts remaining in the trust upon the death of the individual up to an amount equal to the total medical assistance paid on behalf of the individual under a State Medicaid plan.

THE SPECIFIC GUIDELINES FROM SOCIAL SECURITY ARE AS FOLLOWS:

Exception To Counting Special Needs Trust Assets As A Resource

Resources consist of any personal property (cash, real estate, etc.) that a person owns in their name or has any authority to convert the property to cash and is not restricted from using the cash for their own support. Any property not meeting these criteria is not considered a resource. (See page 77, *Frequently Asked Questions*).

In order to exempt assets in a Special Needs Trust from being considered a resource the following criteria must be met in the trust:

— It is established with the assets of an individual under age 65 and who is disabled; or

— It is established for the benefit of such individual by a parent, grandparent, legal guardian or a court; and

— It provides that the State will receive all amounts remaining in the trust upon the death of the individual up to an amount equal to the total medical assistance paid on behalf of the individual under a State Medicaid plan.

Are you wondering what exactly does this mean? It is quite simple. The Special Needs Trust is designed to receive, hold, invest and disburse assets and income for the supplemental needs of your loved one. This will continue for his or her lifetime. The assets in the Trust are exempt from being counted as a resource. Therefore, it will not interfere with your loved one qualifying for SSI and Medicaid.

After your child dies, the remaining assets in the Special Needs Trust will be distributed to whomever you choose. However, before that happens, the State Medicaid program will reclaim an amount equal to the cost of healthcare services provided to your loved one during his or her lifetime. The State must be listed as the first payee and have priority over payment of other debts and administrative expenses.

This is not such a bad deal when you consider that your loved will be able to:

— Remain eligible for SSI and Medicaid

— Have protected assets

— Have trustees appointed by you

— No Medicaid payback during your child's lifetime.

Here is an example:

The Robert Jones Irrevocable Special Needs Trust dated: 6/15/01	$450,000
Total Lifetime Medicaid Benefits to Robert Jones Payback Amount	<u>65,000</u>
Amount left for distribution to remaindermen	$385,000

The Special Needs Trust provision addressing this item varies between states. It is recommended that you follow the steps in (**"Hint 10"** - **Planning, Signing, Checking For Compliance**). Social Security also notes that labeling the trust as a Special Needs Payback Trust, OBRA 1993 Payback Trust, etc., is not sufficient to meet the requirements for this exception. The trust must contain language substantially similar to the language on the previous page.

A result of this change is that the beneficiary of the trust (person with special needs) may now deposit their own assets, including their SSI check, directly into the Special Needs Trust. (Caution: read *The*

Three Year Look Back Rule in Chapter 5 - Social Security Government Benefit Entitlements on page 72). This could not be done with Special Needs Trusts established prior to January 1, 2000 because there was no payback requirement as long as the beneficiary did not deposit his or her own assets. The OBRA Special Needs Trust was used to hold the assets of the person with special needs in order to remain eligible for government benefits.

These regulations should in no way discourage you from creating a Special Needs Trust. The benefits far outweigh any negatives.

Special Needs Trusts Established Before January 1, 2000

Prior to January 1, 2000, Special Needs Trusts created by parents, grandparents, legal guardians or the courts were not required to have a Medicaid payback provision. After the death of the beneficiary (person with special needs), the remaining assets in the Trust were distributed to whomever the creators of the Trust designated. If the beneficiary contributed any of his or her assets to the Trust, then it would trigger a payback because of the commingling of family and beneficiary's assets. In order to avoid this problem, the OBRA Special Needs Trust was created in 1993. It allows a person to put their own assets into this Trust excluding them as a resource. These assets could stem from gifts, inheritance, income, and legal settlements. The person could then qualify for SSI and Medicaid assuming that they met the other requirements. The OBRA Special Needs Trust has a payback provision.

Please turn to page 121, and read
**INCLUSION OF THE PAYBACK PROVISION IN
SPECIAL NEEDS TRUSTS DATED AFTER JANUARY 1, 2000.**

HINT ⭐10

PLANNING, SIGNING, CHECKING FOR COMPLIANCE

It is critically important that you have your Special Needs Trust checked for compliance in your state by both Social Security and Medicaid. State Medicaid agencies vary in what they want stated in the Special Needs Trust. If a family established a separate Special Needs Trust prior to January 1, 2000, they would need an OBRA Special Needs Trust, drafted separately, to receive assets in the name of the person with special needs. If they have a Special Needs Trust established after January 1, 2000, the OBRA Special Needs Trust is not necessary. Assets of the person with special needs may be deposited into the *Living* Special Needs Trust dated after January 1, 2000. Remember, you cannot make any deposits into a Testamentary Special Needs Trust (See page 56 Option 3 - Testamentary Special Needs Trust). Since the "payback" provision applies to Trusts dated after January 1, 2000, it does not matter if assets of the person with special needs and others are commingled. Louisiana, for example, has a "forced heir law" that does not allow you to disinherit children. Assets passed to a person with special needs in their name must be transferred again to an OBRA Special Needs Trust if the family has a Special Needs Trust dated prior to January 1, 2000 (See Option 5, Page 57). Regardless of which state you live in, Special Needs Trusts established after January 1, 2000 may receive assets from the person with special needs since there is a payback provision. In Louisiana, a child will still inherit property directly, however you no longer need to create an OBRA Special Needs Trust to receive inheritance separately.

Parents may make gifts to the Irrevocable Living Special Needs Trust, that they establish, during their lifetime. Regardless of who prepares and executes your trust, have it checked by the appropriate government agencies and get a statement of compliance in writing.

Many families have told me that they previously met with one or more attorneys in order to have a Special Needs Trust drafted. Some completed the process and many did not. Why? Because they did not have total confidence in the attorney and felt that the trust was not done properly.

There is a simple way to eliminate this concern and be assured that your Special Needs Trust is in compliance.

Social Security and Medicaid will review the Special Needs Trust. However, there is a specific process to follow. Neither of these agencies will review a draft of a Trust or one that does not have any assets in it. In order to have a Social Security Regional Center legal department review your trust you must follow the *STEPS FOR SUBMITTING A SPECIAL NEEDS TRUST FOR SOCIAL SECURITY AND MEDICAID COMPLIANCE REVIEW*. Ask your state Medicaid office what you need to do in order to have your trust reviewed.

The reason for this is that if you are applying or if your loved one already is receiving SSI and Medicaid (it does not matter if they are over or under age 18), these agencies will want to know how much money is in the trust and if it is in compliance.

STEPS FOR SUBMITTING A SPECIAL NEEDS TRUST
FOR SOCIAL SECURITY AND MEDICAID COMPLIANCE REVIEW

1. Meet with an attorney to plan your Special Needs Trust.

2. After making sure the Trust meets with your approval, sign it and have the attorney notarize it.

3. Have other legal documents *(Wills, Living Revocable Family Trust, Power of Attorney, etc.)* prepared and executed at the same time.

4. Call the IRS or submit an SS-4 form to get a Federal Tax ID number for the trust. Their phone numbers vary by region.

5. Next, open a savings account in the name of the Special Needs Trust using the tax ID number received from the IRS. Then put $50 in it. You now have a funded living trust.

6. Submit the trust to Social Security and Medicaid and request a letter of compliance. If your child is not on any government programs, you will need to file an application in order to have the trust reviewed.

7. If either agency reports a problem with the trust wording you and/or your attorney may go back to Social Security. They do not typically tell you what is specifically wrong unless you ask. In order for your attorney to act in your behalf, you must provide written authorization. Social Security will provide you with the necessary form *SSA-1696-U4, Appointment of Representative.* There are attorneys who specialize in representing clients in matters pertaining to Social Security. Their fees are regulated and are typically 25 percent of what they recover for you or $4,000, whichever is less.

8. Contact the attorney who prepared the trust to either have it amended or completely redrafted. Since the attorney is responsible to prepare a proper document, there should be no charge for this service. It is recommended that you tell the attorney that you plan to have the Special Needs Trust reviewed and make sure that he or she will make any changes at no additional charge. The attorney may submit the documents to the proper agencies as a service to you. If the attorney already has an approved Special Needs Trust available, ask for a copy of the letter of compliance. Be sure to check the date it was reviewed. You want to make sure that it was reviewed *after* January 1, 2000. It is unlikely that your attorney will not want to cooperate. However, if he or she balks, consider seeing someone else.

In order to avoid any chance of your loved one receiving assets directly in his or her name through a Will or another type of trust, you should specifically state this in these documents. Even though a Will or Trust says, "I leave nothing to William Smith," be assured that he is not being slighted or disinherited. The assets intended for William will be directed to his Special Needs Trust. Grandparents, aunts, uncles and siblings all should include this in their legal documents because it is possible that the person with special needs could automatically receive assets through the family line of succession for inheritance.

HINT

CRUMMY TRUST PROVISIONS

This is a common provision in trusts. However, it should not be included in a Special Needs Trust. The Crummy Provision allows the beneficiary of a trust to withdraw deposits made to the trust by a third-party, within the first 60 days of the deposit. The problem is that with this provision giving the beneficiary the right to remove these assets during the 60 day period, the assets are considered to belong to the beneficiary and will result in the Trust not being in compliance and the assets reclaimable by Medicaid. It could also result in the ineligibility or termination of SSI and Medicaid benefits.

 STORY 8 — *Protecting The Residence*

Debbie, who has Down Syndrome, has lived in the same house with her parents since her birth 61 years ago. Her Dad passed away and Mom, at 84, was not in good health. Debbie had an older brother who also passed away. Mom wanted Debbie to live in their home after she died. She is able to do most things for herself, but needs assistance with finances and "managing the big things." With proper assistance and supervision, she could live in her parents home independently. Her parent's home and contents were their only assets.

Mom died without a will or any other planning. The home was passed to Debbie and her brother's surviving daughter in equal shares. Debbie's niece had no relationship with her. When she learned that she inherited half the house, she wanted it sold for her share of the money. Debbie was forced to move to a group home because there wasn't enough money to buy another house or to buy her niece's share. In addition, Debbie had to repay Medicaid for services provided from the cash she received. Had her parents prepared Simple Wills and left the home to a Special Needs Trust, Debbie could have lived there indefinitely. If her parents wished, the home could pass to their granddaughter after Debbie's death. A 61 year old adult with special needs should not have to be uprooted from the only home she has known shortly after her Mother's death. Debbie had to deal with unnecessary stress and disruption in her life. This did not have to happen.

Making Changes In Your Special Needs Trust

Even though the Trust is irrevocable, you may be able to change the Guardians, Personal Representatives, Trustees, and Remaindermen. If you want to make changes in your Special Needs Trust, it may be more practical to create an entirely new one. You can do the following. First, do not do this on your own. Have an attorney assist you. Once the new trust is created and signed, be sure to do the following:

1. Amend your Will to leave assets to the new Special Needs Trust, instead of the old one.

2. Change the beneficiaries in your life insurance, annuities, and pensions to the new trust.

3. Notify family and friends to also amend their legal documents, insurance policies and pensions plans.

4. If the old trust is currently funded, check with your attorney and Social Security on transferring assets to the new trust (see page 53 **Hint 12**). Have your attorney ask Social Security about using a "Letter of Clarification" to explain the intentions of the existing Special Needs Trust. This could avoid the need to draft a new one.

5. Have the new trust checked for compliance, even if it is basically the same as the old one. Especially if the old trust was dated prior to January 1, 2000.

EXAMPLE:

OLD TRUST: R. Jones Special Needs Trust, dated: September 1, 2002

NEW TRUST: R. Jones Special Needs Trust, dated: June 15, 2007

(As you can see in this example, the date of the trust is important. To avoid any confusion, you may wish to change the name of the trust entirely).

HINT ⭐12

TRANSFERRING ASSETS FROM ONE
SPECIAL NEEDS TRUST TO ANOTHER

If it becomes necessary for you to replace a Special Needs Trust for any reason, you must be careful with the steps you take in transferring assets from a previously established and funded Special Needs Trust.

1. Since the Special Needs Trust is irrevocable, you cannot revoke it. However, you can change your Will and beneficiary designations, leaving assets to the new established Trust.

2. When terminating or withdrawing the assets from a Special Needs Trust, the remaining funds would be given to the Remaindermen, not the beneficiary (person with special needs). If the Special Needs Trust you are withdrawing assets from was established prior to January 1, 2000, there is no payback to Medicaid. If the Special Needs Trust is dated after January 1, 2000, there may be a payback required. This should be checked with Social Security and Medicaid before making any changes. Your attorney may recommend petitioning the courts to transfer assets without any payback.

3. If the assets in the Special Needs Trust are withdrawn, they must be given to the named Remaindermen. The Remaindermen would then "gift" the assets to the new Special Needs Trust. The Remaindermen are under no legal obligation to make the "gift." In order to be assured the transfer will proceed as you want, you may want to change the Remaindermen in the current Trust and name yourself, if you already have not. This way you receive the assets and "gift" them to the new Trust without depending on others.

4. If there is a relatively small amount of money in the existing Special Needs Trust, you may elect to spend it on items or services for the beneficiary to simplify matters. The old Special Needs Trust remains unfunded and inactive.

Choosing Your Trustee(s)

Follow the same method used in choosing Guardians when appointing Trustees. If you decide to use a financial institution (Trust Company, Bank, Brokerage House) it is important that you do the following:

1. Make a list of institutions you are considering.

2. Find out if they manage Special Needs Trusts (not all do).

3. Contact the institutions and ask what is the **minimum** amount of funds they will take under management. This is important because the institution could refuse the trust account or the fees may be too high taking most of the trusts' income.

4. Make an appointment with their Trust department representatives.

5. Inquire as to how many Special Needs Trusts they have, and what is the total amount of assets currently under management.

6. Ask how long have they been managing Special Needs Trusts and what rate of return on investment they have had the last five, ten, twenty years or more.

7. Ask how long have the Trust Officers been with the institution and what is their experience.

8. Ask what services they provide that are included in the fees and what optional services are available.

9. Will they allow you to appoint a "Co-Trustee" to serve and what degree of authority would they accept? The "Co-Trustee" could be a trusted friend or family member with limited authority. You could authorize the "Co-Trustee" to move the Trust account to another "qualified" institution if the current one provides poor service, low return on investment, or the Trust Officer you enjoy working with moves to another institution. You can put certain restrictions on the person moving the account as it pertains to where the assets are placed.

10. There should be **no charges** by the Trust company until the trust is funded and they are managing it. You will probably be the Trustee of the Special Needs Trust during your lifetime and the institution typically does nothing until they succeed you and/or your "Co-Trustees." As the Trustee, you may place assets of the

Trust in accounts to be managed by the Trust company strictly as independent financial advisors with no authority over the Trust. Fees for this service are typically separate from Trust management.

Asset Distribution Options

There are various ways you can plan for the distribution of assets and the financial future of your loved one with special needs.

OPTION 1 - *Irrevocable Living Special Needs Trust (Stand Alone)*

This is the most commonly used and flexible type of Special Needs Trust for the following reasons:

A. "Stand Alone" means that it is a separate document, not part of another trust.

B. The trust is "Irrevocable" meaning that the trust may not be changed or modified and the assets placed in the trust do not belong to the beneficiary when properly worded.

C. "Living Trust" means that it exists now and can be funded at any time. It means that you, family and friends may make gifts to the Trust for your child without jeopardizing any government entitlements. Trust assets may be used at anytime, at the Trustee's discretion for the supplemental needs of the beneficiary.

D. Anyone may make a gift to the Trust. **If the trust was established prior to January 1, 2000, the beneficiary should not contribute any of their personal assets at any time.** If your loved one deposits their own assets (gifts, stocks, SSI checks, etc.) into the Trust it will not result in a payback to Medicaid during their lifetime. However, at their death, Medicaid can claim that since they commingled their assets in the Trust they have the right to the payback. Any assets in your loved one's name now or in the future can be left to an OBRA Special Needs Trust (See *Option 5, page 57). Special Needs Trusts established after January 1, 2000 must have a payback provision included. This authorizes the payback to Medicaid.*

E. Assets you can use to fund the trust may include: savings; life insurance; investments; pensions; real estate; annuities; personal property; etc.

OPTION 2 - *Leave Assets For Your Child To Another Family Member*

You could exclude the person with a disability and leave the share you would have given them to another child, family member, or friend instructing them to use the money to take care of their brother or sister. Of course, the person who receives the money would not be legally obligated to use it for that purpose. This could cause a number of problems. Although designated to provide for their sibling with special needs, these assets legally belong to the person in whose name they are given. Even if they were very conscientious and trustworthy, they might:

1. Be sued by someone and lose the money in a judgement or settlement;
2. Get a divorce, and lose the money in the divorce settlement;
3. Die before the child with a disability dies, and, if they have not made a careful estate plan of their own, the money will go to their surviving spouse and/or children who would not be obligated to provide for the person with special needs.

OPTION 3 - *Testamentary Special Needs Trust*

This Trust does not go into effect until after your death and becomes a matter of public record. The Testamentary Trust cannot have assets placed in it until after your death. Therefore, it would not be available during your lifetime to use as a financial management tool for your loved one or as a means for other people (e.g. grandparents and other extended family) to make gifts to your loved one. In addition, if a change occurred in Social Security law that eliminated the utility of a Special Needs Trust, you might lose the opportunity the Trust provides. Usually when federal law is changed, people who have already acted upon the earlier law are "grandfathered" in. This means an existing, funded Special Needs Trust would probably continue to be legally enforceable for the purposes it was created. A testamentary provision in a living trust would probably not be grandfathered in the new law.

Testamentary Trusts provide no income or estate tax savings as all assets remain in your name until your death. Since the Testamentary Trust is usually part of a Will, if the Will is challenged the trust may never be funded.

OPTION 4 - *Living Family Revocable Trust With Special Needs Provisions*

The Living Family Revocable Trust is a traditional estate planning instrument that provides potential estate tax savings and exempts the funding assets from having to go through Probate. Note that this is a "Revocable" trust and the assets placed in it are considered to belong to the named beneficiaries. It is critical that the attorney drafting this document knows and understands what he or she is doing. This is also a "Living" trust which means it can be funded and used now. Typically the Special Needs provisions don't go into effect until after both parent's deaths. Therefore, the Special Needs portion is more of a Testamentary type trust (see page 56 *Option 3)*. It is important that the person with special needs be specifically excluded as a beneficiary of this trust other than the Special Needs Provisions.

OPTION 5 - *OBRA (Omnibus Reconciliation Act) Special Needs Trust*

This trust was created to allow the person with special needs to transfer any assets in their name including: personal property; real estate; legal settlements (past and future) into a trust to remove the assets from their name in order to qualify for government cash and healthcare benefits. This particular trust must have a "payback" provision because at the beneficiary's death, Medicaid may claim reimbursement from the remaining assets. After the government is repaid, whatever is left goes to whomever you designate (Remaindermen). Although the payback may not sit well with many, it is a small price to pay when you consider that the money is safe and available for your loved one during their lifetime.

If the family has an OBRA Special Needs Trust established prior to January 1, 2000 this trust may still be used to hold assets that were in the name of the person with special needs. This would avoid commingling of funds and triggering the payback provision. Considering that all Special Needs Trusts established after January 1, 2000 must have the payback provision, the OBRA Trust is no longer necessary in any state including Louisiana.

OPTION 6 - *Pooled Trusts*

There are families who have no one to act as a Trustee and do not have enough assets for an institution to manage the trust. An alternative known as a "Pooled Trust" is designed to help these families. These types of trusts can vary from state to state. They are trusts established and managed by non-profit institutions or organizations that pool together the assets of different individuals into one large Master Trust. It operates like a bank where the Master Trust is the bank that manages the deposits of its customers. Your loved one would receive income for life.

In order to remain SSI and Medicaid eligible the Pooled Trust must meet the following conditions as stated by Social Security:

★ The Pooled Trust is established and maintained by a non-profit association;

★ Separate accounts are maintained for each beneficiary, but assets are pooled for investing and management purposes;

★ Accounts are established solely for the benefit of the disabled individual;

★ The account in the trust is established by the individual, a parent, grandparent, legal guardian, or a court; and

★ The trust provides that to the extent any amounts remaining in the beneficiary's account upon the death of the beneficiary are not retained by the trust, the trust will pay to the State the amount remaining up to an amount equal to the total amount of medical assistance paid on behalf of the beneficiary under a State Medicaid plan. This simply means that after your loved one's death, any remaining assets in the Pooled Trust are subject to payback Medicaid. Your child has a separate account of his or her own in the Pooled Trust. If the amount due Medicaid is greater than the amount remaining in your child's trust account, the other funds in the Pooled Trust are not liable for the payback. Your child's assets in the Pooled Trust are not subject to payback Medicaid for another person participating in the trust.

STORY 9 — *Using An OBRA Special Needs Trust*

The following story applies *only* if there is an existing Special Needs Trust established prior to January 1, 2000. (As Special Needs Trusts established after January 1, 2000 may commingle assets of family and the person with special needs, this same procedure could also be used to transfer settlement dollars into it).

There were complications when Tom was born resulting in severe brain damage. He would require 24 hour skilled care for the rest of his life. Tom's parents, Phil and Marcy, filed a malpractice suit and received a multi-million dollar settlement for Tom. The money was placed in a custodial account and a third-party trustee was appointed. Phil and Marcy felt secure that Tom's lifetime needs would always be guaranteed by the settlement dollars. There were a couple of concerns to address that could result in the loss of all the settlement money.

Statistically, most of these large settlements are gone within seven years even though they are intended for a lifetime of care. Life Care Planning professionals will estimate the costs of care for a person and present their findings to the court to be used in determining the settlement amount. The problem arises immediately. Suppose the estimate for lifetime care is $5,000,000 and the court awards this amount. First the attorney is entitled to his or her fee, typically 30 to 40 percent. The recipient's Life Care Plan is now underfunded by $1,500,000 - $2,000,000! In addition, since this money is in a custodial account, it is considered an asset of the person. The result is no SSI or Medicaid. The person may qualify for SSA or SSDI (see page 63 Chapter 5).

You may be thinking, "Okay, so Tom received $5,000,000. What does he need with SSI and Medicaid?" I agree that the SSI cash benefit of a few hundred dollars a month is not important in this case, however, Medicaid is critical. If Tom's parents die before retirement, he will lose his parent's group health insurance after three years

(C.O.B.R.A. See page 64 Chapter 5, "Hint 13"). The only coverage available will be Medicare which won't start for 25 months. Additionally, it does not cover prescriptions. After my discussion with Tom's parents, we all agreed that it was important to be sure that Tom would qualify for Medicaid.

Phil and Marcy hired an attorney who petitioned the courts and were granted approval to create an OBRA Special Needs Trust. The assets in the custodial account, as well as future installment payments, were transferred to this trust. The result was removal of the assets from Tom's name which enabled him to become eligible for Medicaid. A medical crisis for Tom could deplete his settlement in the "blink of an eye." Phil and Marcy had addressed and resolved a potentially devastating issue.

The Three Year Look-back Rule (See page 72) was applied in this case resulting in Tom having to wait three years for Medicaid eligibility. Since he had adequate private coverage through his parents, this posed no problem.

Attorneys have differing opinions as to why they create a Testamentary Trust versus a Living Trust. Living Trusts are more liable to scrutiny by government agencies for compliance than a Testamentary Trust and this is one of the main reasons attorneys prefer Testamentary Trusts. That's fine, however, if the Testamentary Trust does not fit your needs, what good is it even if it is perfect? Be sure that the Trust you establish for your child is right for him or her.

STEP 8 — PUT ALL DOCUMENTS IN A BINDER

Place all pertinent information (*Letter of Intent*, Legal Documents, etc.) in a binder and let those who will take over the care and supervision of your child know where to find it. Provide copies of relevant information to current and future care providers now. Copies of legal documents should not be placed in the binder unless it is stored in a fireproof safe or file cabinet.

STEP 9 — HOLD A MEETING

Give copies of relevant documents and instructions to family and care providers. Review everyone's responsibilities and make sure they understand and agree. This is the time for them to ask questions.

STEP 10 — REVIEW YOUR PLAN

As your loved one grows and changes, so will their needs. It is for this reason that you should review the plan at least once a year. If necessary, make changes in the *Letter of Intent* and consult with an attorney if legal documents need to be modified.

Once families make a commitment to prepare a plan for their loved one by following this process, they can complete it in a very short time and with minimal expense. With this information, families learn why it is important and how they can accomplish this endeavor. What greater gift to give your child than your continuing love and guidance through a comprehensive plan that takes effect when you are no longer here or able.

C H A P T E R   F I V E

Social Security Government Benefit Entitlements

Social Security impacts every part of the planning process. Whether drafting the *Letter of Intent*, creating Wills and Special Needs Trusts, or calculating the monthly budget, it is important to ask yourself, "How will Social Security affect the planning steps I take, and how will my actions impact Social Security benefits?"

Before you take any steps, make a list of your questions. Call Social Security and either ask your questions on the phone, or make an appointment to go to a local office to meet with an advisor. You might want to get the name of the person you will be meeting with and send him or her your questions before your appointment.

As benefits and regulations frequently change, it is recommended that you contact Social Security for clarification and questions. Their services are free of charge. Call Social Security at 800-772-1213 or you may visit their website at **www.ssa.gov**. This website has detailed information on the subjects covered in this chapter.

There are three basic Social Security cash benefits (SSI, SSA, SSDI) and two medical care benefits (Medicaid and Medicare). This chapter will give you a general overview of some of the Government benefits that are available; how to coordinate them with your planning; and how to make sure your legal documents and other planning are in compliance with Social Security and state guidelines.

H I N T ⭐**13**

PRIVATE MEDICAL COVERAGE

Continuing medical coverage is a critical concern. For many, Medicaid or Medicare is the only healthcare plan they qualify for, or that is available to them. Children are typically covered on their parents health insurance policies until they are age 19 or remain full-time students. Then they are on their own. Children with special needs may remain on their parents group insurance (check with your insurance company if you have an individual policy) indefinitely as long as a parent is employed. If the parent changes jobs, group coverage is continuous with no pre-existing condition exclusions with the new employer's plan. If an employed parent dies, their surviving spouse and children may continue the parent's group medical plan for up to 36 months. This benefit is through C.O.B.R.A. regulations and does not apply to all employers. Check with your employer to see if they participate.

If a person with special needs is gainfully employed on a full-time basis, they are entitled to all the employer sponsored fringe benefit programs that their fellow employees have available to them. It is the employer's responsibility to make sure that employees are notified and enrolled. However, it is suggested that the person with special needs request details on all available plans. This includes group medical insurance, dental, retirement plans, and long and short-term disability. Insurance companies may not selectively discriminate.

SSI (Supplemental Security Income)

A. The person applying for benefits need not have any previous employment or they may have an insufficient work history. This is actually to their advantage.

B. The person is 18 years old and the disability can begin at any time and the disability has a prognosis of lasting at least another 12 months. Children under age 18 may qualify for SSI and/or Medicaid based on family income and assets.

C. The applicant may not have more than $2,000 of countable assets in his or her name.

D. When qualifying for SSI the person also qualifies for Medicaid. Some states may require you to file a Medicaid application.

E. The only benefits to be provided with SSI funds are the necessities: food, shelter, and clothing. Duplicating these needs with other funds could jeopardize the person's eligibility. If you are not sure, call Social Security first before making a purchase with Trust or SSI funds.

F. The person's *earned* income sources cannot exceed $780 per month (as of 2002). Their *unearned* income may not exceed $565 per month (as of 2002). If the person has both earned and unearned income, you should discuss this matter with Social Security and Medicaid.

G. If the applicant earns more than $780 per month, they will be ineligible for SSI cash benefits, however, they may continue Medicaid coverage at their own expense (about $50 per month). This makes it possible for people with special needs to earn more income without the threat of losing their medical coverage.

H. If your loved one is denied benefits, you may appeal. When approved, payments are made retroactively to when you first applied.

H I N T

14

HOME AND AUTO OWNERSHIP WHILE ON SSI

An earlier "Hint" explained that a person on SSI and Medicaid could own their own home and remain eligible for benefits. Another asset they may own is a motor vehicle. This is an item that you do not want owned by, or in the Special Needs Trust. If there is an accident and your child is at fault, the injured can sue the "owner" of the vehicle. If the Trust is the owner, it is liable and the assets in the trust will be exposed to litigation and may have to pay a settlement. To avoid this situation, have your loved one own the vehicle and make sure they carry a sufficient amount of liability coverage. The Special Needs Trust will not be vulnerable if you do it this way.

SSA (Social Security Survivor/Retirement Benefits)

A. If a parent dies, reaches retirement eligibility or becomes disabled prior to their Social Security retirement age, all surviving children up to age 18 (with or without a disability) are entitled to benefits.

B. A person with special needs may collect SSA after age 18 for life.

C. There is *no* $2,000 asset limit requirement to qualify.

D. When qualifying for SSI, the person also receives Medicare. However, there is a 25 month waiting period before Medicare benefits begin. (If the person is no longer eligible to receive SSI and Medicaid, and they have to wait for Medicare, private insurance is essential. This is when the C.O.B.R.A. continuation becomes so valuable).

Social Security exempts certain property in the name of the person with special needs. This includes the person's residence and land it occupies; an automobile (usually); up to $1,500 for a burial plot (same benefit for a spouse); and life insurance up to $1,500.

Do not deposit any Social Security Cash Benefits;
checks made payable to your child; or any assets belonging
to your child directly into the Special Needs Trust
*if it was established **prior to January 1, 2000.***

Regardless of when a Special Needs Trust is established, if the beneficiary of the Special Needs Trust directly deposits assets in his or her name into the trust, they will now be considered commingled with other assets. At the beneficiary's death, Medicaid may claim payback from the remainder of the trust.

H I N T 15

HOW TO PROPERLY PLACE SSI CASH IN THE SPECIAL NEEDS TRUST
ESTABLISHED PRIOR TO JANUARY 1, 2000

If you want to save your child's SSI check and provide support the following is suggested:

1. Representative Payee (the person authorized to manage the SSI for the person with special needs) deposits the monthly check into a custodial checking account, *not* into a checking account in the name of the Special Needs Trust. If you are charging your child rent (see "Confirmation Letter"), it should be paid from the SSI checking account.

2. The SSI cash benefit is to be used for food, shelter, and clothing. Thus, you can charge rent. The rest of the money should be used to reimburse the care providers for food, clothing and other necessities.

3. When your child is over age 18 you may reimburse yourself for any expenses you incur on behalf of your adult child. Therefore, you may take the balance of the SSI cash and write a check to yourself. Keep records of the expense and make sure you list only necessities; not movies, videos, vacations, etc.

4. Since this money is a "reimbursement" it is not taxable as income to you.

5. This money is now yours to do with as you wish. One option is to gift it to an account in the name of the Special Needs Trust. It is a gift from you, not a deposit from your child.

6. If someone writes a check to your child, have them make a new one payable to the Special Needs Trust.

STORY 10 — *Grandma's Savings Bonds*

Tom was a month away from his 18th birthday. His parents, Joanne and Mark, called Social Security to schedule a telephone interview to apply for SSI. They were confident that Tom met all the eligibility requirements for SSI and Medicaid. The interview went smoothly. Joanne and Mark completed the necessary paperwork.

A few weeks later they received a letter from Social Security denying benefits to Tom because he had assets in excess of $2,000 in U.S. Savings Bonds. Joanne and Mark had never purchased any bonds for Tom, so they were sure it was a mistake. They called Social Security who confirmed through Tom's Social Security number that he indeed had these bonds.

The logical assumption was, "Who purchased these bonds for Tom?" Joanne's first call was to her Mother. She did not have to go any further. Grandma had purchased over 45 $100 U.S. Savings Bonds in Tom's name with her named as Custodian.

This story is an example of why it is so important to communicate to family and friends that they should not make any large gifts directly to, or in the name of the person with special needs. This mistake is often made with UGMAs (See page 75 Uniform Gift to Minors Act), which allows a tax favored growth on funds put aside for children. This money becomes their's when they meet the age of majority in their state. This creates the same problem as in the preceding story.

SSDI (Social Security Disability Income)

A. A person must have an employment history.

B. To fully qualify, they must have worked 20 quarters of the most recent ten years and have been gainfully employed for about half this time.

C. There is *no* $2,000 asset limit requirement to qualify.

D. When qualifying for SSDI, the person also gets Medicare, however, there is a 25 month waiting period before Medicare provides benefits.

E. The disability prevents the person from earning over $780 per month.

If your loved one is a full-time employee and meets the qualifications for SSDI, they will receive this benefit instead of SSI if they are unable to work under Social Security's definition of disability.

Medicaid & Medicare

Medicaid is a healthcare program funded by both the Federal and State governments. It is intended for certain low-income and needy people including persons with a disability, children, the aged, and blind who meet certain eligibility requirements.

Medicare is a Federally funded healthcare program for some people with disabilities under age 65; people age 65 and older.

Continuing Medicaid After A Parents Death

QIT - Qualified Income Trusts (Also Known As A Miller Trust)

The following case study shows how the QIT (Qualified Income Trust) is used in helping to continue Medicaid benefits after the death of a parent. *(Note: This Trust should not be confused with, nor is it an alternative or substitute for the Special Needs Trust which is discussed in Chapter 4, Step 7, page 42).*

Billy is 34 years old. He receives SSI and Medicaid. His father, Don, dies at age 57. Billy will now be covered by SSA and Medicare. His monthly SSA benefit of $1,800 is based on Don's income and benefits. Your first reaction might be that this is not a bad change. Billy's 2002 SSI income is $545 per month. This means an increase of $1,255 per month or $15,060 per year plus Medicare. Not a bad deal. Or is it? Billy's SSI and Medicaid benefits terminate with his qualification for SSA and Medicare.

PROBLEM:

Medicare has a 25 month waiting period before coverage begins. This plan is not as comprehensive as Medicaid. A major factor is that there is no prescription coverage.

SOLUTION 1:

Check with Don's employer and find out if they offer continued group insurance coverage with the same benefits through C.O.B.R.A. If they don't, the insurance offers the opportunity to convert to an individual policy. This coverage is typically very expensive with limited benefits. In either case, the family pays the full premium.

SOLUTION 2:

If there is a surviving parent who is employed and has group health insurance available through his or her employer, they may enroll their child and are guaranteed acceptance. If there is no more than a 60 day period without coverage, the new insurance picks up where the former carrier leaves off. The surviving parent could seek full-time employment with a company that offers group health insurance benefits if they have no other recourse.

SOLUTION 3:

Contact your State Medicaid office and ask about continuing healthcare plans that are available to a person who transitions from SSI and Medicaid to SSA and Medicare. Be sure to tell them that your loved one qualified for SSI and Medicaid due to a developmental disability. Each State's plans and eligibility requirements differ from one another. Make sure you obtain information from your current state of residence and any future state where your loved one may reside.

PROBLEM:

> Your loved one's SSA income may exceed the maximum income allowable for state Medicaid benefits making him or her ineligible. The deceased parent's employer may not offer continued C.O.B.R.A. coverage.
>
> The individual conversion policy or the C.O.B.R.A. coverage through the group insurance company may be too expensive.
>
> The surviving parent is unable to be employed.

SOLUTION:

> The Qualified Income Trust {QIT}(also known as a Miller Trust) is a Trust that is designed to allow people, who exceed the maximum income limit, qualify for Medicaid. This is not the only requirement for eligibility. The person applying must not have personal assets in their name over $2,000. Creating the Trust and making sure it is in compliance involves income and resource tests and the correct drafting of the document.

The type of healthcare plan offered, the income limits and the eligibility requirements typically differ between states. You should contact your state Medicaid office and use Billy's story as an example to learn about their plan. Besides explaining their requirements and the QIT, they will have printed information to send you, or it may be posted on their website. Don't forget to check with any other state Medicaid office where your loved one may live.

THE THREE YEAR LOOK-BACK RULE

A person with a disability may transfer any of their assets into a Special Needs Trust if it is established after January 1, 2000. The trust must have a payback provision in it as discussed in Chapter 4, Step 7, page 42. Social Security has a "Three Year Look-Back Rule." If a person transfers assets from their estate in order to qualify for government benefits, they would have to wait three years before being eligible to receive Social Security cash benefits. This does *not* apply to a person with a disability transferring their assets to a Special Needs Trust. The person would be eligible immediately, if they meet all requirements for SSI cash benefits. This is not necessarily the case with Medicaid. That decision lies with the State. You should contact your State Medicaid office and find out about their specific guidelines. If your child will be living in another state, after your death, don't forget to check with their Medicaid office.

One of the most important concerns families have for their loved one with special needs is continuing medical coverage. It is critical that your child have medical coverage through another source if he or she must wait three years for Medicaid to begin. There are ways to do this. Turn back to page 64 ("**Hint 13**" - **Private Medical Coverage**), for guidance on how you can avoid a situation where your child has no medical plan.

SOCIAL SECURITY SSI

Application Process, Charging Rent, and the Confirmation Letter

About six to eight weeks prior to your child's 18th birthday, call the Social Security Administration at: 1-800-772-1213 to schedule a telephone interview to apply for SSI and Medicaid (the name may differ in your state) benefits. You may also apply online at:

www.ssa.gov/applyforbenefits.

After the interview you will receive a form which needs to be completed. You will need the following information before you apply. If you are unable to provide all that is required Social Security will assist you. Do not delay filing your application.

★ Social Security Number

★ Birth Certificate or proof of age

★ Residential information: Address/Mortgage/Lease/Property Owner/Rental Amount

   Don't forget the Confirmation Letter (next page)

★ Payroll slips, bank accounts, insurance policies, burial fund records, all other information about your income and property

★ Names, addresses, and phone numbers of doctors, hospitals, and clinics that have provided services

★ Proof of U.S. citizenship or eligible non-citizen status

★ Checkbook account for direct check deposit.

You will be asked where your loved one is going to live. If he or she is living at home with you, they will want to know if you are charging rent. If you do not charge rent, the SSI benefit will be reduced by one-third (1/3). The amount of rent you are required to charge is based on the total household expenses divided by the number of occupants.

EXAMPLE:

Household Expenses =	$2,100/month
Divide by # of Occupants (3) =	700/month

You would be required to charge $700 per month rent even though the maximum SSI monthly benefit may be less. In addition, rent is income and taxable to you. That means an additional $8,400 per year of income in this particular example.

By submitting the following **Confirmation Letter** with your application forms (*and tell the interviewer as well*) you can reduce the rent you charge to as little as $150 –$300 per month. Discuss with Social Security what you feel the value of the benefit received is in order to establish a figure in this range.

CONFIRMATION LETTER

Date:

Social Security Administration

Address

City/State/Zip

RE: Confirming Statement for Room & Board Payment

    Name:

    Social Security # :

To Whom It May Concern:

This is to confirm that the room and board being charged to the above named person, my son/daughter/other in the amount of $(insert amount) per month, is the same that I would charge to any boarder regardless of whether or not they are related to me. He/she/other is a separate economic unit from our household. I am the owner and rent liable person for the dwelling unit.

Sincerely,

Your name

Address

Phone

UGMAs, UTMAs, AND 529 PLANS

How They Affect Social Security Benefit Eligibility

The UGMA (Uniform Gift to Minors Act) was established to allow the title to property to be passed to minors without the need of appointing a guardian or creating a trust. The type of property that can be passed is limited to personal property including cash, annuities, and securities. While the minor child has legal ownership of the property, he or she may not receive it directly until reaching the age of majority in their state of residence. The age of majority varies between states. The UTMA (Uniform Trust to Minors Act) is the successor to the UGMA. It expands the type of property that can be transferred to a minor. Check with your State's specific guidelines on what property qualifies.

During the period of time that the UGMA/UTMA is in your minor child's name, it will not be counted as their resource. Therefore, it will not interfere with a minor child qualifying for SSI or Medicaid. The problem occurs when your child with special needs reaches their age of majority (18 in most states). Upon reaching the age of majority, all the UGMA/UTMA assets pass directly to your child in their name. The amount will probably exceed $2,000. This will result in your child being ineligible for SSI or Medicaid. In addition, the Medicaid payback could be enforced if your child was covered as a minor. If your child has an UGMA/UTMA now and you terminate it, Social Security can use the "Three Year Look-Back Rule" and deny Medicaid benefits for that time frame.

This situation with UGMAs and UTMAs creates a dilemma. On the one hand, if your child with special needs may have the potential and ability to attend college, but it is too soon to know, what can you do to enjoy the benefits of a tax favored savings program for their future education? If they are unable to continue their education after public school and you want them to be SSI and Medicaid eligible, it is better not to create an UGMA or UTMA. There is another option that will allow you to put aside money for your child's education. If they do not use it, it can be used for another child.

The program that eliminates the previous concerns and penalties with UGMAs and UTMAs is called a 529 Saving Plan. Earnings in a 529 plan are exempt from federal taxes if spent on college costs which include tuition, books, and residency until the year 2010. They will continue if the current tax law is renewed. These plans vary dramatically among the States. You are not required to buy your State's plan. You may investigate the benefits of plans in other states. Some states have a matching grant or scholarship program and many exempt the earnings on withdrawals from being taxed. These plans offer greater flexibility as to where you invest the money.

Let's suppose that your child with special needs will not be attending college. What happens to the money in the 529 Plan? The money can only be used for college. You can change the beneficiary of the plan to another child for their education. It is very important that you obtain the specific information for 529 Plans in your state and any other state your child may live in after your death. The 529 Plan can be used for any child's education, not necessarily your own.

★ ★ ★

FREQUENTLY ASKED QUESTIONS ABOUT SOCIAL SECURITY

What determines whether or not someone is eligible?

Social Security uses a three-pronged test to determine whether or not a person is disabled as defined in the statute. First, one must have a physical and/or mental impairment. Second, that impairment must prevent a person from doing any substantial gainful activity. Third, the impairment must be expected to last at least 12 months or result in death.

What must one do to collect benefits?

Meeting the SSA definition of disability is not all it takes to qualify for benefits. Each Social Security program has its own additional requirements.

What are the additional requirements to collect Social Security disability?

To be eligible for SSDI benefits, one must have worked and paid Social Security taxes. SSDI is like an insurance program. One must have paid a "premium" in order to be insured. The "premium" is what is taken out of a paycheck as FICA or the Social Security taxes paid directly if one has been self-employed. With a few exceptions, a person is fully insured if he or she has at least one credit for each calendar year beginning the year after they turn 21 and before reaching age 62 or became disabled.

How many credits must one have?

A minimum of six credits is always required. A person has disability insurance status if he or she has at least 20 credits during a 40 quarter period ending with the quarter the individual is determined to be disabled.

When one meets the SSA definition of disability and has enough credits to have disability status, when do they begin receiving checks and medicare coverage?

There is a five month waiting period after the disability begins before receiving SSDI benefits. Medicare benefits begin with the 25th payment month.

How much money will a person receive from Social Security?

Social Security has a complicated formula to determine the actual amount of your benefits. The size of the check is based on a person's average indexed monthly earnings.

Do family members qualify for benefits?

Auxiliary benefits may be payable to family members on the earnings record of a person entitled to disabled worker's benefits. This includes: 1) unmarried children under age 18 or 19 if in high school full-time; 2) unmarried children age 18 or older if they have a disability which started before age 22; 3) a spouse who is age 62 or older, or any age if caring for a child who is under age 16 or disabled.

What if a person is disabled and does not meet the SSDI work requirement?

A person may qualify for Supplemental Security Income or SSI benefits. SSI is a program which was designed for those 65 and older, disabled or blind who have little income and/or resources.

What counts as income?

Social Security considers both "earned income" and "unearned income." Earned income includes wages, salary, and earnings from self-employment. This category also includes sheltered workshop pay, sick pay or short-term disability payments during the first six months of stopping work, royalties and honoraria.

What counts as unearned income?

Unearned income includes "deemed income," in-kind support and maintenance, SSDI, Social Security retirement, Veteran's Administration (VA) pensions and compensation, state welfare payments, death benefits from life insurance, rents, dividends, and interest.

What forms of income do not count?

Social Security does not count the value of food stamps and the value of federally subsidized housing. The first 20 dollars of income from most sources is not counted. The first 65 dollars of earned income does not count and is known as the "earned income exclusion." One-half of any other earned income is also not counted. There are also exclusions for IRWEs and a special rule for student income.

What are IRWEs?

IRWEs are Impairment-Related Work Expenses which are expenses for items that a person must purchase for work because of their disability.

How does summer employment affect students?

There is a special rule for student income, provided that the student is under the age of 22 and is disabled or blind and regularly attends school. Check with Social Security for the current income limits.

How does SSI consider resources?

As with almost everything else Social Security has defined "resources." Eligibility for SSI is based on financial need. An individual may not own non-exempt resources exceeding $2,000.

What is a resource?

A resource is property which is both owned by the individual and available to him or her. The applicant must have the right, authority or power to liquidate the resource for it to be considered available.

Does Social Security count all resources?

Social Security exempts or excludes some resources, such as:
1. Residence (if the person lives there)
2. Household goods and personal effects up to $2,000 in value
3. The full value of an automobile used for essential daily activities (i.e. work, doctor visits, etc.)
4. Life Insurance with no cash value
5. The total value of a person's or their spouse's life insurance policy if the value does not exceed $1,500
6. A burial fund of up to $1,500 in value for the person and spouse. This may be affected by life insurance policies.

What about tools and office equipment?

Social Security also exempts resources that a person with a disability uses to produce extra income and resources excluded under a Plan for Achieving Self-Support (PASS). Plan For Achieving Self-Support is a program for achieving self—support. It is a plan for the future. Many people with disabilities want to work, but maybe they need to go back to school before they can get a job. Or, maybe they would like to start their own business, but don't have the money. Whatever their work goal may be, a PASS can help reach it. The person with special needs must have a goal to have a job that will produce sufficient earnings to reduce their dependency on SSI. Contact Social Security directly or their website for detailed information.

What options are available if the person meets all the requirements for SSI, but whose countable resources exceed $2,000?

When a person's resources exceed $2,000 they will not be eligible for SSI, and in most cases, Medicaid. One can convert assets to exempt status by:

1. Purchasing a more expensive home or modifying their existing home to accommodate their needs

2. Purchasing a vehicle

3. Paying off the mortgage or other debts

4. Purchasing personal goods

5. Pre-paying for final arrangements

6. Creating a Special Needs Trust and transferring resources into the Trust

7. Qualified Income Trusts (Miller Trusts) can be used after the death of a parent where SSA income benefits exceed the state's maximum.

Should one consider converting resources in order to qualify for SSI?

SSI provides an individual with a limited income benefit and Medicaid coverage. There are a few states where SSI eligibility does not mean automatic eligibility for Medicaid. If no other healthcare benefits are available privately, Medicaid eligibility makes converting resources worthwhile.

Are there options when one needs SSI & Medicaid but fails the income test?

1. Make sure that all income exemptions and exclusions are properly taken.

2. Have expenses paid directly to providers (cable TV, cleaning, etc.).

3. Have the person pay rent to avoid reduction of SSI cash benefits (See page 74 *Confirmation Letter*).

4. If the person has a *Special Needs Trust*, be certain that it is properly administered. Food, shelter or clothing should not be provided by the Trust. Cash distributions should not be made to the Beneficiary.

Does Social Security's definition of disability differ for children?

Yes. An adult must have a mental or physical impairment that keeps them from "substantial gainful activity" for at least a year or will result in death. A child cannot be evaluated using work-related criteria. Social Security has a "Listing of Impairments" in their regulations.

What if the condition does not appear on the "list"?

Social Security formerly used a "comparability" standard. With the enactment of the "Welfare Reform Act of 1996," this method has been changed.

How has this changed?

The new law eliminates the comparable severity standard. Instead, it provides that a child under 18 would be considered to have a disability if he or she has a medically determinable impairment which results in marked and severe functional limitations and which can be expected to result in death, or which has lasted or can be expected to last for a continuous period of not less than 12 months.

The new law also eliminates references to maladaptive behavior in the domain of personal/behavioral function in the "Listing of Impairments" and to discontinue the use of an individualized functional assessment in evaluating a child's disability.

How does Social Security determine a child's disability?

The combined effects of all physical and mental impairments of a child are to be considered in determining whether a child is disabled. Social Security regulations provide for the evaluation of children who cannot be tested because of their young age.

What other factors does Social Security consider?

Most children under 18 do not have their own income and do not have many assets. However, when children live at home (or are away at school, but return occasionally and are under parental control), Social Security considers the parent's income and assets when deciding if a child qualifies for benefits. This process is called "deeming."

What happens when a child with special needs turns 18?

The parent's income and assets are no longer considered for the child's continued eligibility for benefits. However, if the child lives at home with his or her parents they must pay rent or their SSI benefit could be reduced by one-third. Parents should consider charging rent. (See page 74 *Confirmation Letter*).

What should you charge for the monthly rent?

Social Security will tell you that an individual should pay a "fair share" of household expenses. This is typically the number of people residing in the house divided into the total expenses. This amount could exceed the monthly SSI check. The "Confirmation Letter" can be used to charge a monthly rent as little as $150 - $300.

What should you do with the rental income received?

This money is yours to do with as you please. You may deposit it into the *Special Needs Trust* you create.

How is SSI affected by assets in a trust?

The *Special Needs Trust* is a discretionary trust. When properly drafted, assets funding the Trust are not considered those of the Beneficiary. Most trusts do not provide this protection. The Trust may have unlimited assets and is not restricted to the $2,000 resource maximum limit.

How does money distributed from the Special Needs Trust affect SSI payments?

Money paid directly to providers for items other than the person's food, clothing and shelter do not reduce SSI payments. Items that are eligible to be paid by the Trust are medical care, telephone bills, education, etc. If providers are paid directly for food, clothing and shelter from the Trust, this will reduce the SSI payment and may end SSI eligibility. Money paid directly to the Beneficiary in excess of acceptable levels reduces the SSI payments.

Can an adult, disabled since childhood, collect Social Security benefits?

They may be eligible for SSA (Social Security Survivors/Retirement Benefit) when either parent collects retirement or disability benefits or dies. Eligibility for this benefit includes Medicare.

When a person is determined to have a disability, are they eligible for Social Security for life?

Social Security has systems that monitor individuals over time. The individual may periodically be required to submit current medical information. Many persons with disabilities are able to return to work. Social Security offers various return to work incentives.

C H A P T E R   S I X

Choosing Qualified Advisors

Attorneys - Financial Advisors - Insurance Agents

Another obstacle to planning for families is trying to find qualified professionals who have experience and expertise in Special Needs Planning. As with any type of advisor, there are those who think or say they know what they are doing, but have little or no understanding of this type of planning. Whether the advisor is trustworthy, ethical and/or means well, if they are not knowledgeable on this subject, you and your loved one are going to suffer the consequences from their mistakes and incorrect advice.

Do not think that because an advisor has a professional certification such as: Attorney; CPA (Certified Public Accountant); CLU (Certified Life Underwriter); CFP (Certified Financial Planner) etc. that they are competent and qualified to do Special Needs Planning. The studies involved in earning these designations does not include those related to Special Needs Planning. These people may be experts in their fields, but may not be able to help you meet your goals and your loved one's needs. I have heard some excellent presentations from professionals in these fields speak at conferences, and many who have no business speaking on this subject at all.

There are financial companies who have formed non-profit organizations in order to offer their planning services. I am not implying that they are doing anything wrong. However, it has always bothered me when a company or individual does not come right out and say who they are, what they are doing, and what products they are selling. One insurance company offers "free planning" through their "non-profit organization" and conveniently fails to mention that they earn their income by selling insurance and investment products. It takes me a minimum of ten to 12 hours to assist a family individually in planning. I can't imagine a professional who can afford to spend the required amount of time doing this work for free or having to rely on families buying their products in order to be compensated. Clients of mine, attending one of these sessions, spent the entire evening trying to get the speaker to tell him how they earned their income if they were doing planning for "free." At the end of the two hour seminar, the presenter finally told the audience that she sold insurance products. There should be nothing to hide or be ashamed of. A true professional should be proud to tell people what they do and how they earn their income. An attorney, financial advisor or insurance agent, who is knowledgeable and understands all the issues that need to be addressed with Special Needs Planning is invaluable. I cannot think of a more affordable and better way of funding your loved one's needs than with life insurance and sound financial investing. However, it is important that you buy what is right for your loved one's plan, not what someone wants to sell you because they can make a bigger commission on another type of insurance plan or because the investment recommended is an "in-house" type that pays them a bonus.

It is important to remember that none of these advisors is paying you for the privilege of working for you. You are the one paying for services. No one should tell you what to do. You tell the advisors what you are trying to accomplish. It is their responsibility to assist you in attaining what *you* want, not what they *think* you need. You are the boss. You write the check. You do the hiring and firing. If you are not comfortable with the person you interview, find someone else!

When you find a qualified special needs attorney, they may very likely be able to refer you to financial advisors and insurance agents with experience in this field. You may check with other families in your community or support groups. Contact the local Arc (Association for Retarded Citizens), your State Bar Association, case worker, local support group, etc.

The decision is yours. You may elect to hire an advisor to do all your planning, or you may elect to do most of it yourself and have these advisors take care of the legal work and designing the way you will fund your plan. *The Special Needs Planning Kit©* provides you with the ability to put your own plan together with legal and financial assistance (see Chapter 8 for details).

Do not let yourself be discouraged. There are qualified and trustworthy professionals who are dedicated to making sure that your loved one's plan is secure and fulfills your goals.

Questions To Ask Before You Choose Your Advisors

Most advisors offer an initial consultation without any obligation. The following are suggested questions to ask these advisors during the first interview. Formulate other questions from this book to check and see how much the person knows and if you will be comfortable and confident working with him or her.

1. What experience do you have in planning for a person with special needs?

2. How long have you been providing Special Needs Planning services?

3. What portion of your time is dedicated exclusively to Special Needs Planning?

4. Are you paid through fees and/or compensated by selling products?

5. What are your typical charges for services and what does it include?

6. How many clients with special needs do you have?

7. May I call any of these families for a reference?

8. Are you affiliated with companies whose products or services you sell?

9. Which charitable organizations are you affiliated with as an active member?

10. What organizations, support groups, agencies and families can provide references?

11. Do you have professional credentials specifically related to this field?

12. How many plans do you do each month?

13. How long does it typically take to complete a plan?

14. What other advisors do you work with (financial, tax, legal, insurance)?

15. What is their expertise?

H I N T

RECORD MEETINGS WITH ADVISORS

You will be covering a great deal of information with your advisors. It is impossible to remember everything. It is suggested that you record your meetings in order to be able to have everything that was discussed available for reference and review. Be sure to ask the advisor prior to the meeting for permission.

Do not be shy about asking questions. This is too important to hold back. Your child's future depends on you. If you do not ask, you will never be sure. The result is that you will probably not begin or complete a plan. If you are uncomfortable asking the potential advisor directly, send them these questions and ask for a written response. Could it be any easier? Do not let this obstacle remain as an excuse not to plan.

C H A P T E R   S E V E N

Insurance: Selecting The Best Policies To Fit Your Needs

Working with a competent insurance agent or financial advisor you trust can make a positive and profound impact in helping you achieve your goals for your child. Don't make the meeting with an advisor a contest to see "who wins." If you have the need for more coverage "and don't buy" and the agent "doesn't make the sale," the loser is your family. Prior to becoming a fee-based Special Needs Planner, I was proud that I sold insurance products for 20 years in conjunction with traditional business and estate planning. The key to buying the right policy is to make sure that it fits your needs and budget. What is right for one family may be totally wrong for another.

There are two basic types of life insurance: Term and Permanent (Universal Life and Whole Life). All are fine products when used properly. I recently heard an insurance agent speak at a conference where he told the audience that they should buy Survivor Life (also known as Joint Life or Second To Die Permanent Insurance). This policy has its place. However, I could not disagree more with the agent's recommendation that all families should purchase this plan. Another type of Universal Life policy is Variable Life. Accumulated cash value in these policies is typically invested in the stock market. There are many variations of these policies with alternate investments available. If you choose this type of policy, make sure the death benefit is guaranteed in the policy. Have the agent specifically point it out in a sample policy. Some of these plans have death benefits that may vary with the fluctuation of the stock market. I don't think you would be happy if you bought a $500,000 Variable Life policy and at your death your loved one's received a far lesser amount.

Survivor Life or Second To Die Life Insurance policies are typically used to pay estate taxes after the death of the second spouse. Both Mom and Dad would be covered by the same policy. **There is no death benefit paid at the first spouse's death.** The death benefit is paid after the surviving spouse dies. Let us take a look at a typical situation and see what type of policy is the right buy for this family.

Frank and Louise are 35 years old. They have three children, one of whom has special needs. Frank earns about $55,000 per year and Louise does some part-time work out of their home which adds another $5,000 per year to their income. After completing their family and Special Needs Planning they established that they needed $500,000 of life insurance to meet the income and other financial needs of their children at their deaths. Like most families, money is tight and they are careful about spending.

OPTION 1: Survivor Life Insurance

A. This policy pays *no death benefit* at the first spouse's death. It is not until the second spouse dies that any death benefit is paid.

B. If Frank dies first, Louise receives nothing from this policy and the same for Frank if Louise predeceases him. If Louise survives Frank by another 30 or 40 years or more, the policy will sit in a drawer someplace accumulating cash value and dividends that will not be sufficient to support Louise and her children. What if she survives her child with special needs? What good is this policy then? How do you think Louise would feel, knowing that the money she needs today is sitting in a drawer, unavailable, until after her death?

C. The premium for this coverage will be a few thousand dollars per year. Most likely, this is more than they can afford or should spend on their particular budget.

D. If a family has a large estate that will incur Federal Estate Taxes and they have other life insurance paying an immediate death benefit, then Survivor Life can be a wise purchase. It should not be the primary or only life insurance for most families.

OPTION 2: *Term Life Insurance*

A. Term policies are available as Yearly Renewable Term (premiums increase each year); and or 5, 10, 15, 20, 25 or 30 Year Level Premium periods. The longer the term period the higher the cost. A couple age 35, in good health and non-smokers may each purchase $250,000 of 30 Year Level Term insurance for about $350 - $400 per year per person. This is a fraction of the cost of Survivor Life and pays a death benefit when the first and second spouse dies.

B. At either Frank's or Louise's death, the surviving spouse immediately receives $250,000 to be used as the survivor sees fit. At the surviving spouse's death, the remainder of the $250,000 and the death benefit of $250,000 from the second spouse's death can all pass to the Special Needs Trust or be divided amongst the surviving children (excluding the child with special needs directly).

C. An argument against purchasing Term Insurance is that you are "renting" instead of "owning" your policy. If the policy expires and you still need coverage, it will be substantially more costly as you get older. You must also meet medical requirements. If, however, you are disciplined and prudent, your investments; pension plan; home equity and other assets may be adequate to provide for your loved one. Hopefully, your other children will be independent and not rely on you for financial assistance.

D. Most Term Insurance policies allow you to convert to a permanent policy at a later time. You can convert in various increment amounts without providing any evidence of insurability. This means no physical examination or medical history required and provides the opportunity to change to permanent coverage when you can afford it and want it.

OPTION 3: *Permanent Insurance (Universal and Whole Life)*

A. If you can afford the cost, permanent insurance is ideal as it will insure you for your entire lifetime. It does not run out like term. An individual policy on each parent will provide immediate benefits at either death as illustrated above in Option 2.

B. Depending on the type of Permanent insurance you purchase, these policies will accrue cash value, dividends, and/or interest. This coverage provides more options and flexibility than Term insurance. It is recommended that you discuss this with a qualified agent or financial advisor.

OPTION 4: *Other Types of Insurance Coverage*

A. Disability Income insurance replaces your income if you are unable to work due to an illness or injury. If your income stops, how will you support your family and be assured that your plans will be attainable? Do you think that your Social Security Disability Income will be sufficient? This coverage is available through employer group plans or individual policies.

B. Long Term Care Insurance covers the costs of a nursing home stay and avoids family assets being wiped out to provide care in later years. Many policies offer home care options.

C. Group/Individual Medical Coverage may be continued indefinitely for a person with special needs. Check with your employer or the insurance company before your child leaves the public school system, and/or turns 19. If your child is not now on your group insurance, you may be able to add them to your coverage. You may have to provide medical evidence, however, your child cannot be declined. If they have had other group insurance at least 60 days prior to applying for the new group insurance plan, there is no pre-existing condition exclusion or waiting period.

D. Full-time employees with special needs may *not be discriminated against.* They are entitled to every employer sponsored group fringe benefit and are guaranteed to receive them. They include medical, dental, short and long-term disability, pension plans, etc. Employers must comply with regulations and guidelines for coverage.

E. C.O.B.R.A. is a benefit that allows continuous group medical coverage. The spouse and children of a deceased employee may continue this coverage for up to three years. If your loved one has to wait 25 months for Medicare, this coverage would fill that gap. Those continuing coverage must pay the full cost. You don't have to cover all dependents. You can elect to cover the person with special needs only.

F. Waiver of Premium

This benefit is sometimes included or available as an option on policies. If the insured should become temporarily or permanently disabled, they will not have to pay any insurance premiums after a set waiting period and until they recover. After recovery, they do not have to payback waived premiums. This benefit varies in policies and between insurance companies.

Your insurance agent and/or financial advisor plays a key role in guiding you on how to fund and make your plan secure. Check with any potential agents before you work with them as to what they charge for their services. Most work solely on commission. Rate quotes are available on the internet. However, it is important to work with someone to be sure that everything is set up correctly including the right policy, beneficiary designations, ownership, etc.

Make sure that any representations made by an agent are backed up in writing. You may also request the agent's state license number and check with your Department of Insurance regarding the status of the agent with whom you plan to work.

C H A P T E R   E I G H T

The Special Needs Planning Kit ©
Solutions for Your Loved One - Peace of Mind for You

Now that you have completed reading *The ABC's of Special Needs Planning Made Easy* ©, your next step is to decide how you want to plan. If you have unusual or complicated circumstances, it may be necessary for you to have someone assist you from start to finish. Refer to page 85 Chapter 6, Choosing Qualified Advisors. This will guide you through the selection process. The majority of families who read this book will be able to do most of the planning on their own by using *The Special Needs Planning Kit* ©.

Planning for the future well-being of a person with special needs can be overwhelming, to say the least. That is why I created the Kit. It is an easy to use and complete, step-by-step guide to making sure that all the needs of your loved one—regardless of age or type of disability—are met in the event you are unable to care for them in the future.

Based on my experience assisting thousands of families throughout the U.S. since 1993, I realized the need for a simple, comprehensive, and affordable way for families to plan. The Kit is designed to include every possible issue families must face, from legal planning to government benefits to making sure your loved one's favorite snacks are in the fridge. Instead of concerning yourself with where to begin, who to turn to, or issues of time or cost, you can take the necessary steps to assure your loved one a life of security, care, supervision, and quality.

The Special Needs Planning Kit © has detailed instructions for recording information for Wills, the Special Needs Trust and other legal documents as well as the *Letter of Intent*.

A legal planning section includes instructions for your attorney on how to coordinate the Special Needs Trust, a draft of which is included in the Kit, with other legal documents. Fees for services can vary greatly. Another option for legal services are membership legal organizations. They provide attorney referrals in your area through their membership program who will prepare Simple Wills and notarize the Special Needs Trust. Your monthly membership fees (usually $12 - $16) may include these services at no extra charge. One company is the Legal Club of America. You may visit their website at **www.legalclub.com** for information about their services and membership fees. After you receive your membership confirmation, you call their toll free number and you will be referred to a local associate attorney, in or near your community, who will notarize your Special Needs Trust and prepare your Simple Wills. This and other resources provided are independent companies. They are not affiliated with, nor are they endorsed by Bart Stevens Special Needs Planning.

With the Kit you will receive the *Letter of Intent* forms in which you write all the information future care providers will need to continue the same level of care and supervision you yourself have provided. The Kit also contains a section on government benefits and information on guardianship.

A computer disk is provided which includes all the forms in the Kit.

The costs for this type of planning by professional advisors including attorneys, financial advisors, tax consultants and insurance agents can easily exceed $2,500. *The Special Needs Planning Kit* © is available for $240. By providing this information to your legal and financial advisors, it should result in less of their time required and lower fees.

THE SPECIAL NEEDS
PLANNING KIT ©

SECTION 1 — Introduction

Special Needs Plan Summary

Making the Process Simple

Information to Family & Friends on Gifts & Inheritance

Beneficiary Change Instructions

Step-By-Step Instructions Through Completion

Annual Review Checklist

SECTION 2 — Life Plan Data

The Life Plan Data Forms - How To Begin

Step-By-Step Guide & Sample Case Study

Life Plan Data - Worksheets & Official Forms

SECTION 3 — Legal Planning

Understanding The Special Needs Trust

Estate Planning Terms & Questions

The Special Needs Trust

Information for Local Attorneys

Special Needs Trust - Final Steps to Completion

Guide to Special Needs Trusts

SECTION 4 — Letter of Intent

Letter of Intent for Special Needs - Overview

Letter of Intent Forms

SECTION 5 — Government Benefits

Social Security SSI & Confirmation Letter

Frequently Asked Questions

SECTION 6 — Choosing Attorneys, Guardians, & Trustees

Simplifying the Legal Process

What to Provide to the Attorney

Designating Guardians & Trustees

Here are just a few comments from Mom's and Dad's who have purchased *The Special Needs Planning Kit ©*:

"I've known for years that I need to make arrangements for when I'm gone. As a single parent you're faced with so many day to day "chores" that the thought of completing a future plan for your child is absolutely overwhelming. As I started to do the plan, each step was broken down with such easy to follow directions and examples that it only took me a few hours to complete it. I feel the weight of the world is off my shoulders. If I can do it, other families can too."

— *Sue Peterson - Glendale, AZ*

"Everything we needed to know was clearly laid out in the excellent resource binder. All we had to do was fill in the blanks."

— *Ellen and Mark Gross - Falls Church, VA*

> *Mark Gross is an attorney with the Justice Department and served on the President's Council on Mental Retardation. Ellen Gross is an attorney and Associate Director of "Community of Caring," a project of the Joseph P. Kennedy Foundation.*

"It's something that has to be done. Bart has organized the process in easy step-by-step directions."

— *Russ & Mimi Laney - Snellville, GA*

Resource Information

Of the millions of families who have a loved one with special needs, it is estimated that less than 15 percent have any contact or involvement with the thousands of special needs support groups and agencies throughout the country. They are the best "resource centers." Obtaining support and information are two critical issues. Parents of recently diagnosed children will find a wealth of knowledge and experience amongst the member families in their community. I see this first hand at my workshops. As the group of attending families get to know one another through their questions and comments to me, they soon begin exchanging information with each other. Who better to speak with than the parents of another child with a disability. There is so much you can learn from each others experiences.

Local, State, and National Conferences offer excellent opportunities for families to learn and share. They have sessions addressing many subjects related to medical treatment and advances, therapies, legislation, special needs planning, government benefits, etc. In addition, they provide a wonderful social experience. My conference speaking engagements have taken me to New Orleans, New York City, San Diego, Walt Disney World, and Nashville. For many of the families attending, it is the only opportunity they may have to visit and enjoy these places. Another benefit of traveling this way is that there are typically hundreds of families at these conferences. You will find that there are better accommodations and more services ready and available for the special needs of your loved one.

It is not difficult locating these organizations. Ask anyone providing services to your child including their teacher, case worker, physician, therapist, etc. They will know because they are probably working with many similar families. The internet is an incredible source. You know the routine. Get on line and enter your loved one's disability in the search engine.

Following is a list of a few organization and informational websites to help you get started. These sites also have links with many other information and resource websites. They also list and link with your local chapter of these organizations.

AAPD
AMERICAN ASSOCIATION FOR PERSONS WITH DISABILITIES
1819 H STREET NW, STE. 330
WASHINGTON, DC 20006
PHONE: 202-457-0046
TOLL FREE: 800-840-8844
WWW.AAPD.COM

AAMR
AMERICAN ASSOCIATION ON MENTAL RETARDATION
444 N. Capital St., NW, Ste. 846
Washington, DC 20001-1512
Phone: 202-387-1968
Toll Free: 800-424-3688
www.aamr.org

THE ARC OF THE UNITED STATES
1010 Wayne Ave., Ste. 650
Silver Spring, MD 20910
301-565-3842
www.thearc.org

ASSOCIATION FOR CHILDREN WITH DOWN SYNDROME, INC.
4 Fern Place
Plainview, NY 11803
Phone: 516-933-4700
www.acds.org

AUTISM SOCIETY OF AMERICA
7910 Woodmont Ave., Ste. 300
Bethesda, MD 20814-3067
Phone: 301-657-0881
Toll Free: 800-3AUTISM
www.autism-society.org

BART STEVENS
SPECIAL NEEDS PLANNING
12406 N. 32nd St., Ste. 102
Phoenix, AZ 85032
Phone: 602-404-4239
Toll Free: 888-447-2525
www.BSSNP.com

BATTEN DISEASE SUPPORT AND RESEARCH ASSOCIATION
120 Humphries Dr., Ste. 2
Reynoldsburg, OH 43068
Phone: 740-927-4298
Toll Free: 800-448-4570
www.bdsra.org

BRAIN INJURY ASSOCIATION OF AMERICA
105 N. Alfred St.
Alexandria, VA 22314
Phone: 703-236-6000
Family Helpline: 800-444-6443
www.biausa.org

C.H.A.D.D.
CHILDREN AND ADULTS WITH ATTENTION-DEFICIT/ HYPERACTIVITY DISORDER
8181 Professional Pl., Ste. 201
Landover, MD 20785
Phone: 301-306-7070
Toll Free: 800-233-4050
www.chadd.org

CdLS SOCIETY
CORNELIA DE LANGE SYNDROME FOUNDATION
302 W. Main St., Ste. 100
Avon, CT 06001
Phone: 860-676-8166
Toll Free: 800-223-8355
www.cdlsusa.org

EASTER SEAL SOCIETY
230 W. Monroe St., Ste. 1800
Chicago, IL 60606
Phone: 312-726-6200
Toll Free: 800-221-6827
www.easter-seals.org

EPILEPSY FOUNDATION
4351 Garden City Dr.
Landover, MD 20785-7223
Toll Free: 800-332-1000
www.efa.org

FEAT
Families for Early Autism Treatment
PO Box 255722
Sacramento, CA 95865-5722
Phone: 916-843-1536
www.feat.org

FRAGILE X FOUNDATION
PO Box 190488
San Francisco, CA 94119
Toll Free: 800-688-8765
www.fragilex.org

LDA
LEARNING DISABILITIES
ASSOCIATION OF AMERICA
4156 Library Rd.
Pittsburgh, PA 15234-1349
412-341-1515
www.ldanatl.org

LEGAL CLUB OF AMERICA
8551 W. Sunrise Blvd., Ste. 105
Plantation, FL 33322
Phone: 954-377-0222
Toll Free: 800-305-6816
www.legalclub.com

MARCH OF DIMES
1275 Mamaroneck Ave.
White Plains, NY 10605
Toll Free: 888-663-4637
www.modimes.org

MDA
MUSCULAR DYSTROPHY ASSOCIATION
3300 E. Sunrise Dr.
Tucson, AZ 85718
Toll Free: 800-572-1717
www.mda.org

NATIONAL ASSOCIATION
FOR DOWN SYNDROME
PO Box 4542
Oak Brook, IL 60522
www.nads.org

NATIONAL DOWN SYNDROME CONGRESS
1370 Center Dr., Ste. 102
Atlanta, GA 30338
Phone: 770-604-9500
Toll Free: 800-232-NDSC
www.ndsccenter.org

NATIONAL DOWN SYNDROME SOCIETY
666 Broadway
New York, NY 10012
Phone: 212-460-9330
Toll Free: 800-221-4602
www.ndss.org

NICHCY
NATIONAL INFORMATION CENTER FOR
CHILDREN AND YOUTH WITH DISABILITIES
PO Box 1492
Washington, DC 20013
Toll Free: 800-695-0285
www.NICHCY.org

NORD
NATIONAL ORGANIZATION
FOR RARE DISORDERS
55 Kenosia Ave.
PO Box 1968
Danbury, CT 06813-1968
Phone: 302-744-0100
Toll Free: 800-999-6673
www.rarediseases.org

PACER
PARENT ADVOCACY COALITION
FOR EDUCATIONAL RIGHTS
8161 Normandale Blvd.
Minneapolis, MN 55437
Phone: 952-838-9000
www.pacer.org

PRADER-WILLI SYNDROME ASSOC.
5700 Midnight Pass Rd.
Sarasota, FL 34242
Phone: 941-312-0400
Toll Free: 800-926-4797
www.pwsausa.org

PRE-PAID LEGAL, INC.
321 E. Main Street
Ada, OK 74820
Phone: 580-436-1234
Toll Free: 800-654-7757
www.prepaidlegal.com

RETT SYNDROME
9121 Piscataway Rd
Clinton, MD 20735
Phone: 301-856-3334
Toll Free: 800-818-RETT
www.rettsyndrome.org

SOCIAL SECURITY ADMINISTRATION
Toll Free: 800-772-1213
www.ssa.gov

SOTOS SYNDROME SUPPORT ASSOC.
3 Danada Sq. East, Ste. 235
Wheaton, IL 60187
Toll Free: 888-246-7772
www.well.com.org

**SPINA BIFIDA
ASSOCIATION OF AMERICA**
4590 MacArthur Blvd., NW
Ste. 250
Washington, DC 20007-4226
Phone: 202-944-3285
Toll Free: 800-621-3141
www.sbaa.org

SPECIAL OLYMPICS
1325 G St., NW, Ste. 500
Washington, DC 20005
Phone: 202-528-3630
www.specialolympics.org

**TASH
THE ASSOCIATION FOR PERSONS
WITH SEVERE HANDICAPS**
29 W. Susquehanna Ave.
Ste. 210
Baltimore, MD 21204
Phone: 410-828-8274
www.TASH.org

UNITED CEREBRAL PALSY
1660 L St., NW, Ste. 700
Washington, DC 20036-5602
Phone: 202-776-0406
Toll Free: 800-USA-5-UCP
www.ucp.org

WILLIAM SYNDROME OFFICE
1316 N. Campbell, Ste. 16
Royal Oak, MI 48067
Phone: 248-541-3630
www.williams-syndrome.org

S U M M A R Y

Let's review what you have accomplished by reading this book. You:

★ Know why it is necessary to prepare a plan for your loved one with special needs

★ Are aware of the consequences your loved one faces if you do not plan

★ Can replace the Government Plan

★ Addressed and eliminated the obstacles

★ Have a step-by-step method to follow

★ Understand the benefits of the Special Needs Trust

★ Have a good basic knowledge of the various Social Security benefits

★ Know what types of insurance plans are available

★ Know how to continue private and government healthcare programs

★ Have a process and guidelines for finding and choosing your advisors

★ Have a list of resources for information and support

★ Have the availability of *The Special Needs Planning Kit©* to assist you in preparing a plan on your own and/or with the guidance of your advisors.

Do you think you will ever have a better opportunity to plan than now? You have eliminated the obstacles and excuses. Whatever steps you take in the planning process, continue to use this book as your guide. As you address specific issues, refer to the appropriate chapters in this book. Consider having your advisors and the family members designated as future care providers also read this material. Planning should be a family process, not just for Mom and Dad.

At the beginning of the book I asked you to think about what would happen to your child tomorrow morning if you were no longer here and had done little or no planning. You now know what problems occur and must be addressed. You can take the lead with your family and begin the process.

Your decision to plan now or wait not only affects your loved one, but also the rest of your family. Sure it is a tremendous responsibility. However, it has to be done. Take action now! You *can* do it.

Good luck!

Updates and Revisions

Laws and regulations change. New planning ideas and methods are developed. Readers make suggestions and requests for new and additional information. Your feedback about this book is very important to me. Your comments and suggestions will be appreciated. If you would like to be notified about new information regarding all aspects of Special Needs Planning simply drop us a line or send us your email request. Should you decide to become a member of *The Special Needs Community Network* (See Bart Stevens Special Needs Planning Products and Services on pages 116 and 117) at **www.BSSNP.com** you will receive this information automatically.

GLOSSARY OF ESTATE PLANNING TERMS

Amendment

A change in a Trust Agreement. It should refer to the specific Article in the Trust and must be signed by the Settlor and notarized. An attorney experienced in Special Needs Trusts should be consulted for assistance in making any changes.

Advocate

A person or institution who will serve as a friend and look out for the best interests of the person with a disability. The Advocate is not court appointed. In some cases, where the person can manage most of their own affairs, an advocate from a charitable organization may be more appropriate than a legal Conservator or Guardian.

Beneficiary

The person or institutions who receive the benefit of the Will, Trusts (including the Special Needs Trust), Life Insurance, Annuities, Pensions, and other types of property passed through "Beneficiary Designations."

Codicil

An amendment to a Will. The Codicil is a separate document that is signed with witnesses like the Will, but amends some portions of the Will.

Conservator/Guardian

A court ordered mandate by which an individual or institution is appointed to: (A) manage the estate of the person judged incapable (not necessarily incompetent) of caring for his/her own affairs; (B) be responsible for the care and decisions made on behalf of a person when that individual, again, is determined to be unable to care for himself/herself. A Conservator/Guardian can be appointed to serve in either one or both ways. In some states Guardians assist the person and Conservators assist the estate of the person with special needs. If the parents of a child with special needs want to continue as the legal guardians after their child reaches age 18, they must also petition the courts to be appointed. A person must be at least 18 years of age in order to serve. Guardians may include a relative, friend, government agency, the courts, or a corporation.

The guidelines and regulations pertaining to guardianship and conservatorship vary greatly amongst the states. If your child will live in another state with guardians, get information from that state and your current state of residence. It is strongly suggested that you consult with an attorney regarding this matter.

Co-Trustee

This person or institution serves with the appointed Trustee. They must agree on all decisions pertaining to the Trust.

Discretionary Powers

The authority given to a Trustee to make decisions on the distribution of income and assets in a trust. The person creating the trust defines what the Trustee can and cannot do pertaining to the management of the trust.

Effective Date

This is the date when the Trust Agreement is signed and becomes effective.

Estate

All possessions of an individual at the time of his/her death.

Estate Tax

The federal government and some states assess a tax on property owned at the death of an individual.

Executor/Personal Representative

The individuals or corporations that are appointed in the Will who will have the legal responsibility for carrying out the provisions of the Will to the best of their ability according to the current federal and state laws. The executor may seek the assistance of an attorney to complete the probate process.

Fiduciary

Fiduciaries assume the responsibility of acting on behalf of another individual. There are public and private fiduciaries and it can be a person or an individual.

Grantor/Settlor

The person(s) who create a trust.

Guardian (See Conservator)

Heir

This is the person who inherits property under state law.

Income Beneficiary

Generally, the person in the Trust Agreement who will receive the income from the trust during his or her lifetime.

Intervivos Trust

Also known as a Living Trust. It functions during the lifetime of the Grantor. Assets may be transferred or gifted to the trust during the Grantor's lifetime and assets used for the benefit of the named beneficiary.

Irrevocable Trust

An irrevocable trust means that the items placed in the trust cannot be taken out of the trust except by ending the trust and disbursing the items to the appropriate remainderman. The trust has its own ID number and is taxed as a separate "person." However, income produced by assets in the Trust may be distributed to or used in behalf of the named beneficiary. The Trust is required to file an annual report. The Trustee does have the right to manage the Trust funds by normal prudent man rules of investment.

Letter of Intent

This is one of the most important documents of an estate plan. In this very personal letter, the parents, spouse, siblings, and other care providers express their hopes and desires for the future of their loved one with special needs while also providing detailed information and instructions for the person's care, supervision, and security.

Living Trust

A living trust allows the person who creates it and anyone else to fund it during their lifetime and has the power to allow the named beneficiaries to benefit from the assets in the trust immediately.

Living Will

This provides for the donation of organs at a person's death and also forbids being kept alive by means of life support.

Minor

Any person under the age of 18. Parents have responsibility for their children until age 18 when they legally become "emancipated" adults.

This means that the person is legally responsible for themselves and is no longer under the legal supervision of the parents. The person with special needs may not have the capacity to act as an "adult" and the parents may want to continue in their previous role obtaining Conservatorship and Guardianship.

Per Capita

Means of distribution to Remaindermen without representation. This means that each descendent receives an equal share. If a direct descendent dies before receiving their inheritance, the other named heirs receive his or her portion. In the case of a grandparent leaving assets to their children, if one or more of their children should predecease them, that child's portion goes to the surviving children, not the children of the deceased (the grandchildren).

Per Stirpes

Means of distribution to Remaindermen according to the principle of representation. If a parent leaves property to each child and a child does not survive them, then that child's portion will pass on to their children.

Pooled Trust

The combining of assets of many people into a single trust managed by non-profit organizations. Each person's assets are kept separate. Guidelines and policies regarding these trusts vary.

Power of Attorney - Medical & Legal

A legal document in which an individual appoints another person to make medical and legal decisions on their behalf at a time when the individual is unable.

Probate

The court proceedings in which there is supervision over the property passing from a deceased person to beneficiaries under the provisions of the Will or, if there is no Will, under the provisions of state law.

Remaindermen

The person(s) or institution(s) who will receive the remainder of the Trust after the income beneficiary has died and the Trust ends.

Representative Payee

The person or agency authorized to manage funds provided through Government Entitlements. They are required to provide detailed records of the use of these funds.

Revocable Trust

A Revocable Trust means that the items placed in the Trust can be taken out of the Trust. This type of Trust is taxed as part of the estate of the Grantors. The assets placed in the Trust are considered the property of the named beneficiary.

Special Needs Trust

An Irrevocable Trust designed to provide for the supplementary needs of the person with special needs over and above benefits provided by government entitlements. The trust funds are not meant to supplant or replace government programs. The Trustees should never give funds that would cause loss or reduction of government benefits unless there is an emergency. The assets in the Trust are not considered in the name of the beneficiary. The disbursement of funds is left to the discretion of the Trustee. This type of Trust is not considered an asset for determining government benefits. Only those funds which are actually disbursed directly to the beneficiary will count as earned or unearned income.

Successor Trustee

This person(s) takes over the responsibility of managing the Trust after the death or legal incompetence of the initial Trustee(s).

Testamentary Trust

This type of trust becomes "activated" at the Grantor's death. It cannot be funded during their lifetime as in a Living Trust. This Trust is also a matter of public record.

Trust

A legal entity established either by written agreement signed during the life of the person or by a Will. The Trust is governed by the terms in the written document. It is a contract between the Settlors, the Trustee(s), and the Beneficiaries.

Trust Agreement

The document which creates the Trust.

Trust Corpus

The property and funds held in the Trust. It is also called the Trust Estate.

Trustee

The person(s) who manages the Trust. There is a fiduciary responsibility for seeing that the funds are properly invested and disbursed according to the wishes of the Trustor and the laws of the state. The Grantor and Initial Trustee may be the same person.

Trustor

Also known as the Settlor or Grantor. This is the person who creates the Trust.

Will

The purpose of a Last Will and Testament is to direct the distribution of the assets of the estate to all the beneficiaries. Parents of the person with special needs would exclude naming him or her so they will not receive any portion of the estate in their name which would create assets and; therefore, reduce or eliminate government benefits. This person's share should be left to the Special Needs Trust.

BART STEVENS
special needs planning

P R O D U C T S

THE ABC'S OF SPECIAL NEEDS PLANNING MADE EASY©
— Contact us for bulk orders

THE SPECIAL NEEDS PLANNING KIT©
— Contact us for bulk orders

COMING EARLY 2003 — THE SPECIAL NEEDS COMMUNITY NETWORK
— At *Bart Stevens Special Needs Planning*, our commitment and relationship with the many families in our community does not end when families complete their plan. Rather, it is the beginning of a long-term relationship through the "Special Needs Community Network." We are creating it to provide a place specifically for those who are a part of the Developmental Disability Community. It will be a resource for sharing information, asking questions, updates on changes in future planning, a monthly chat room, and more. This is going to be your "Special Needs Community Network."

THE SPECIAL NEEDS COMMUNITY PIN™
— A unique piece of fine jewelry, you will wear with pride, that represents all those who are a part of the community of people with disabilities.

FOR MORE DETAILS OR TO PLACE YOUR ORDER VISIT OUR WEBSITE AT:
www.BSSNP.com
or call: 888-222-8441

116

BART STEVENS
special needs planning

SERVICES
ALL SERVICES AVAILABLE NATIONWIDE

The Special Needs Trust Draft is included in the fees for all services except the initial consultation. Our fee schedule is posted on our website: www.BSSNP.com or call us toll-free at 888-447-2525

★ **INITIAL CONSULTATION**

This one to one and a half hour consultation provides an opportunity for families to ask questions, review the various planning options, and decide how they would like to proceed. There is no obligation.

— Family receives a copy of *The ABC's of Special Needs Planning Made Easy©*

★ **INDIVIDUAL HOURLY PLANNING ASSISTANCE**

★ **COMPREHENSIVE INDIVIDUAL PLANNING**

Bart works privately with the family throughout the planning process. The "family" includes services provided to grandparents, aunts and uncles, and others involved in the life of the person with special needs. If the biological parents are divorced, planning for both parents individually may require an additional fee.

— The plan is reviewed with the family. Upon approval by the family, documents are sent to appropriate advisors (attorneys, CPAs, financial advisors). Families may work with their own advisors or one of our referrals.

Products and Services

117

— Upon execution of legal documents (Wills, Trust, etc.) we file an SS-4 form for a tax identification number for the Special Needs Trust and file all Beneficiary Change forms for life insurance, annuities, 401(k)s, IRAs, etc.

— Hold final review meeting with family.

— Family receives a copy of *The ABC's of Special Needs Planning Made Easy©*.

★ *ONE DAY GROUP PLANNING WORKSHOPS*

Minimum 25 pre-registered and pre-paid families.

Family receives *The ABC's of Special Needs Planning Made Easy©* and *The Special Needs Planning Kit ©*.

Post workshop assistance is available on an hourly fee basis.

★ *CONFERENCE/SEMINAR SPEAKER*

Contact Kirsten Adams, Marketing Consultant, at: 602-404-4239   Toll Free: 888-447-2525; E-mail: info@BSSNP.com

Available for local, state, regional, national and international events.

I N D E X

INCLUSION OF THE *PAYBACK PROVISION* IN SPECIAL NEEDS TRUSTS DATED AFTER JANUARY 1, 2000

Laws and Regulations are usually subject to different interpretations by various parties. It is not uncommon for this to occur with issues pertaining to Social Security. Such is the case as it pertains to the information addressed in Step 7 – Consider Creating A Special Needs Trust – Special Needs Trusts Established After January 1, 2000 and Exception To Counting Special Needs Trusts Assets As A Resource on page 44.

Social Security's position on this issue is that a Payback Provision must be included in all Special Needs Trusts established after January 1, 2000. If this provision is not included, the assets in the Special Needs Trust will be considered a "countable resource" of the Trust's beneficiary (the person with special needs) and will result in the loss or reduction of both SSI and Medicaid benefits. In discussions I have had with an attorney in Louisiana and two in Arizona, who are well versed in Special Needs Trusts, they do not agree with the interpretation of the regulation and stand by the position that the Payback Provision is not required. It is not my intent to take either side in this matter, but to suggest that you discuss this with your legal counsel for his or her opinion as well as Social Security and your State Medicaid agency. Your attorney may or may not wish to include this provision. Whatever decision you and your attorney make, it is imperative that you follow the instructions in Step 7 - Steps For Submitting A Special Needs Trust For Social Security And Medicaid Compliance Review on page 44 in order to be assured that your Special Needs Trust is in compliance.

If you decide to challenge Social Security in this matter, it will likely result in delaying your loved one's qualifying and receiving SSI and Medicaid benefits for months, years or never. Litigation could result in having to appeal, through the courts, a ruling favoring Social Security's position. You can stand on principle and pursue this through the appeals process, however, it is critically important to consider what effect this will have on your loved one. You must ask yourself and your legal counsel, "Is it worth doing?"

The payback to Medicaid for services provided during your loved one's lifetime is not required until after their death as long as assets are not in your loved one's name and are placed in the Special Needs Trust. Assets placed in a properly drafted Special Needs Trust will be available to your loved one throughout their life. During your loved one's lifetime, their Social Security cash benefits alone could add up to hundreds of thousands of dollars. Potentially far more than any payback amount due Medicaid. The costs in litigating this matter in the courts will be great in legal fees, time and the effects on your loved one. They may exceed any benefits "won" through the legal process. And, you could lose!

Regardless of who is right or wrong or the result of any litigation in this matter, the attorney representing you and those representing Social Security may not necessarily be affected by the decision. However, it will affect you and your loved one.

Read through the information in Step 7 carefully and discuss this with your attorney. Whatever your decision, make sure Social Security and Medicaid have the opportunity to review your Special Needs Trust and provide a Letter of Compliance.

Caution: If you decide to establish a Special Needs Trust without the payback provision, do not put any assets belonging to your loved one with special needs directly into this Trust. Follow the guidelines in this book for Special Needs Trust established before January 1, 2000.